A TASTE FOR T...

A Taste for the Secret

Jacques Derrida and
Maurizio Ferraris

Translated from the French and Italian by
Giacomo Donis
Edited by Giacomo Donis and David Webb

Polity

Published with the financial assistance of the Italian Ministry of Foreign Affairs.

First published in 2001 by Polity Press in association with Blackwell Publishers Ltd.

Editorial office:
Polity Press
65 Bridge Street
Cambridge CB2 1UR, UK

Marketing and production:
Blackwell Publishers Ltd
108 Cowley Road
Oxford OX4 1JF, UK

Published in the USA by
Blackwell Publishers Inc.
350 Main Street
Malden, MA 02148, USA

A catalogue record for this book is available from the British Library.

Library of Congress Cataloging-in-Publication Data

Derrida, Jacques.
    [Gusto del segretto. English]
    A taste for the secret / Jacques Derrida and Maurizio Ferraris ; translated from the French and Italian by Giacomo Donis ; edited by Giacomo Donis and David Webb.
        p. cm.
    Includes bibliographical references.
    ISBN 0–7456–2333–6 (alk. paper)—ISBN 0–7456–2334–4 (pbk. : alk. paper)
    1. Derrida, Jacques—Interviews. 2. Philosophy. I. Ferraris, Maurizio,
1956–   II. Donis, Giacomo. III. Webb, David. IV. Title.

B2430.D484 A513 2001
194—dc21   00–065575

Typeset in 11 on 13 pt Berling
by Graphicraft Limited, Hong Kong
Printed in Great Britain by MPG Books Ltd, Bodmin, Cornwall

This book is printed on acid-free paper.

Contents

Carthaginem quidem cum eloqui volo, apud me ipsum quaero ut eloquar, et apud me ipsum invenio phantasiam Carthaginis; sed eam per corpus accepi, id est per corporis sensum, quoniam presens in ea corpore fui et eam vidi atque sensi, memoriaque retinui, ut apud me invenirem de illa verbum, cum eam vellem dicere. Ipsa enim phantasia eius in memoria mea verbum eius, non sonus iste trisyllabus cum Carthago nominatur, vel etiam tacite nomen ipsum per spatia temporum cogitatur; sed illud quod in animo meo cerno, cum hoc trisyllabum voce profero, vel antequam proferam.

Augustine, *De Trinitate*, 8, 6, 9

And when indeed I wish to speak of Carthage, I seek within myself what to speak, and I find within myself a notion or image of Carthage; but I have received this through the body, that is, through the perception of the body, since I have been present in that city in the body, and I saw and perceived it, and retained it in my memory, that I might find within myself a word concerning it, whenever I might wish to speak of it. For its word is the image itself of it in my memory, not that sound of two syllables when Carthage is named, or even when that name itself is thought of silently from time to time, but that which I discern in my mind, when I utter that disyllable with my voice, or even before I utter it.

Augustine, *On the Holy Trinity*,
trans. Arthur West Haddan, p. 121

Secretaire

A *secretaire* is a writing desk in which papers are locked away. A *secretary* is an assistant, like Theuth with the Pharaoh in the Egyptian story in the *Phaedrus*, or perhaps like Phaedrus himself, who conceals Lysias' speech under his cloak, and again like Phaedrus as a sparring partner – or interviewer – of Socrates. But, by analogy with 'syllabary', 'secretary' could also be a catalogue, even an iconography or a portfolio, or more exactly an *ichnography* in which one collects, writes or describes *traces*, which are, at bottom, *secrets*.

What secrets? More than half of this text is composed of an interview, animated in the last part by the entrance of Gianni Vattimo, as third party in our dialogue. Only the second section is an essay, that is, something that is also considered (too hastily) a monologue. Now, an interview is itself traditionally considered an iconography – one that, through 'live' speech and full phenomenalization, illustrates thought. And to the objection that thought, any thought, is hypotyposis, i.e. sensibilization and phenomenalization, one might reply, with perfectly tranquil ingenuousness, that interviews are all the more iconographic and picturesque because they expose what is hidden in essays, novels or poems.

But here Plotinus' judgement, which we shall have occasion to gloss, comes into play: 'form is a trace [*ichnos*] of the formless', he remarks; which amounts to saying that every *Gebild* and every *Gestalt* is the bearer of a secret. And this applies specifically to interviews, whose rule is perhaps that saying of Bacon's which Kant places at the beginning of the

Critique of Pure Reason: 'De nobis ipsis silemus'. After all, it is not a question of explaining the script with a transcribed speech that is still more phenomenic and clarified. The question, instead, is that of wondering why thought resembles not only what is called the 'life of the mind', but also reality; and above all of questioning the schematism that regulates this 'strange resemblance'.

J.D. and M.F.
Paris, 12 June 1996

'I Have a Taste for the Secret'

Jacques Derrida

I

Form is a trace of the formless; it is the formless that produces form, not form the formless; and matter is needed for the producing; matter, in the nature of things, is furthest away, since of itself it has not even the lowest degree of form. Thus lovableness does not belong to matter but to that which draws upon form: the form upon matter comes by way of soul; soul is more nearly form and therefore more lovable; Intellectual Principle, nearer still, is even more to be loved: by these steps we are led to know that the primary nature of Beauty must be formless.

Plotinus, *Enneads*, VI, 7, 33, trans. S. MacKenna
[translation modified]

Derrida. If by 'system' is meant – and this is the minimal sense of the word – a sort of consequence, coherence and insistence – a certain gathering together – there is an injunction to the system that I have never renounced, and never wished to. This can be seen in the recurrence of motifs and references from one text to another in my work, despite the differing occasions and pretexts – a recurrence that, having reached a certain age, I find rather striking. What I have managed to write in the course of these past thirty years has been guided by a certain insistence that others may well find downright monotonous. 'System', however, in a philosophical sense that is more rigorous and perhaps more modern, can also be taken to mean a totalization in the configuration, a continuity of all statements, a *form* of coherence (not coherence itself), involving the syllogicity of logic, a certain *syn* which is no longer simply that of gathering in general, but rather of the assemblage of onto*logical* propositions. In that case deconstruction, without being anti-systematic, is on the contrary, and nevertheless, not only a search for, but itself a consequence of, the fact that the system is impossible; it often consists, regularly or recurrently, in making appear – in each alleged system, in each self-interpretation of and by a system – a force of dislocation, a limit in the totalization, a limit in the movement of syllogistic synthesis. Deconstruction is not a method for discovering that which resists the system; it consists, rather, in remarking, in the reading and interpretation of texts, that what has made it possible for philosophers to effect a system is nothing other than a certain dysfunction or 'disadjustment', a certain incapacity to close the system. Wherever I have followed this investigative approach, it has been a question of showing that the system does not work, and that this dysfunction not only interrupts the system but itself accounts for the desire for system, which draws its *élan* from this very disadjoinment, or disjunction. On each occasion, the disjunction has a privileged site in that which one calls a philosophical *corpus*. Basically, deconstruction as I see it is an attempt to train the beam of analysis onto this disjointing link.

The insistence I spoke of earlier – that concern for consequence and coherence which, I think, is philosophical – turns, however, against the philosophical as systematic. As a result, insistence leads to difference; that is, to the impossibility of identification and totalization. Mine, then, is an *excessively* philosophical gesture: a gesture that is philosophical and, at the same time, in excess of the philosophical. And this raising of the stakes – how to be more than philosophical without ceasing to be philosophical? – marks with its hubris all the themes I have dealt with.

My principal interests have tended towards the great canon of philosophy – Plato, Kant, Hegel, Husserl; but, at the same time, towards the so-called 'minor' loci of their texts, neglected problematics, or footnotes – things that can irritate the system and at the same time account for the subterranean region in which the system constitutes itself by repressing what makes it possible, which is not systematic. I strategically privileged this confrontation – at once canonical and non-canonical – with the philosophical canon because I found it more urgent and profitable at first. This did not stop me, however, from looking not only at non-canonical texts, but also at non-philosophical ones – literary texts, which I shall come to in a moment.

I think that the case of the imagination is enlightening in many ways. Several things drew me towards the question of imagination, in various forms and languages (imagination in Aristotle is not the productive imagination in Kant or in Hegel). First of all, there is something about it that has made it a threat to truth, intellect and reality – yet a resource as well. It could easily be shown, in fact, in Plato as in others, that imagination has an ambiguous nature: on one hand, it is that which threatens truth and the idea – the image is inferior to the idea; and, on the other, it has a positive function – it is philosophically and pedagogically necessary. It is the locus of fiction, but also of a certain synthesis, a place of mediation – especially in Kant where imagination is precisely the third term, the 'third'. And in the end everything we have said about the system comes down to a question of the 'third'. This third term can be taken as the mediator that permits synthesis, reconciliation, participation; in which case that which is neither this nor that permits the synthesis of this and that. But this function is not limited to the form it has taken in Hegelian dialectic, and the third of neither-this-nor-that and this-and-that can indeed also be interpreted as that whose absolute heterogeneity resists all integration, participation and system, thus designating the place where the system does not close. It is, at the same time, the place where the system constitutes itself, and where this constitution is threatened by the heterogeneous, and by a fiction no longer at the service of truth. What particularly interests me here is that which participates in participation and non-participation. And the regular return to this theme – which is also the theme of art, of mimesis – betrays a double postulation in my work, and a raising of the stakes – since we find at the heart of the third as participation that

which in no case allows itself to be reappropriated by participation, and thus by a philosophical system.

For this reason, I am not sure that something contemporary can be determined, originally, as starting from a certain
date, as if something began after Hegel, with the post-Kantian
or in the post-Hegelian, with Nietzsche. Whatever is modern,
contemporary or new in the history we spoke about a moment ago, from Nietzsche to Heidegger to others, is perhaps
that which becomes contemporary to us in and through the
gesture that revokes or denounces the possibility of a periodization and thus of a contemporaneity in that sense. Fundamentally, Kierkegaard, Nietzsche and others are thinkers of
the untimely, who begin by putting into question the interpretation of history as development, in which something that
is contemporary to itself – self-contemporary – can succeed
something that is past. Paradoxically, the idea of contemporaneity as a relationship reconciled with itself in the 'now' of
a present is in fact a classical idea, and belongs to all that is
not contemporary – from Plato to Hegel; it is precisely what
is put into question by the 'contemporaries'. For Kierkegaard,
Nietzsche, Heidegger, there is no 'now us' – this dislocation,
which may well be more vividly experienced by the philosophers we call 'contemporaries' than by the others, is what
interests me.

'The time is out of joint', says Hamlet. Literally, 'to be
out of joint' is said of a shoulder or a knee that has gone out
of its socket, that is dislocated, 'disjointed'. Thus, time 'out
of joint' is time outside itself, beside itself, unhinged; it is
not gathered together in its place, in its present. Another
translation of *Hamlet*, by Gide, which, it seems, agrees quite
closely with English idiom, says curiously: 'Notre époque est
déshonorée'; and in fact it appears that, in a tradition that
goes from More to Tennyson, 'out of joint' was used in a
moral sense, and meant disorderly, corrupted, unjust. 'The
epoch is disorderly, not as it ought to be, "ça va pas".' It is
this 'ça va pas' that gives rise to the desire not only for
adjustment, but for justice. Now, with this in mind, if we
reread Heidegger's 'The Anaximander Fragment', we shall
find a very strange and powerful meditation on *dikē* and

adikia. Heidegger seeks to demonstrate that, primarily, *adikia* does not have a moral or juridical sense, the sense of 'injust-ice' that Nietzsche and others attach to it. *Dikē* and *adikia* need to be understood in a sense prior to the moral or juridical, namely as that which is, or which is not, *aus den Fugen*, 'out of joint': *dikē* is jointure, *adikia* is the disjointed. Heidegger poses the question: How can present beings (*ta onta*), which are out of joint, render justice (*dikē didonai*, according to the Anaximander fragment)? In other words – and it is here that Heidegger poses basically the same ques-tion as Plotinus before him, and Lacan afterwards – how can one give what one does not have? Which is to say: how can that which is disadjusted render justice, or, more precisely, jointure, *Fugen*? Heidegger interprets all this in terms, on the one hand, of time, present being, *on*; and, on the other, in terms of *Fugen*, the jointure of times.

To return more schematically to the terms of our question: that which is heralded or gains urgency in the contemporaries we have evoked is perhaps just this dislocation of the present, which renders the present non-contemporary to itself and these people non-contemporary to one another, without that relationship with history and time which the classical philo-sophers thought they had. These contemporaries are thus not contemporary at all, and they oblige us to interpret the history of philosophy in a far more troubled and suspicious manner. I have often posed questions about the way in which Heidegger uses the concept of 'epoch'; in any case, what attracts me to these contemporary thinkers is not their contemporaneity but, somehow, the opposite: it's a certain malaise about belonging to a time, to our time – the diffi-culty of saying 'our' time. Our time is perhaps the time in which it is no longer so easy for us to say 'our time'.

Ferraris.   How does writing enter philosophy? I'm not at all convinced by the generally accepted version of this entrance, which holds that, after 'the end of metaphysics', philo-sophers no longer dealt with truth, but limited themselves to a sort of social welfare service based on conversation. This is a dogmatic assumption, because I don't think you can say

that there is a metaphysics 'as such', let alone that it is subject
to generation and corruption. Unless by 'metaphysics' you
happen to mean those English advertisements like the one
Hegel mocked in the preface of the *Encyclopaedia*, which
promised 'The Art of Preserving the Hair, on Philosophical
Principles'. At times it is also a question of the cunning of
a repressive tolerance, which authorizes philosophers to do
whatever they wish, with the exception of their proper work,
which is the search for truth. The recourse to language has
certainly played a major role, because, in appearance, saying
that 'language speaks' seems to reduce philosophy to the
vainest of conversations; while it is noteworthy that the
sense of a philosophy (think, for example, of the Aristotelian
tradition) may at least partially survive even the most tortuous
of transmissions, which is not the case with literature, where
a very great deal is lost in translation.

Derrida.   Writing did not 'enter' philosophy, it was already
there. This is what we have to think about – about how it
went unrecognized, and the attempts to repudiate it. Basically, the difference between the two forms of writing in
Plato, between *hypomnēsis* and *anamnēsis*, was a dispute not
between speech and writing but rather between two different
writings, one bad and the other good. Good writing is thus
always *hanté* by bad writing; and this 'haunting' relationship
prevents us from thinking of the relation between philosophy
in general and writing in general as an exteriority of any kind.

But conversely, for the reasons I have just indicated, among
the 'contemporaries' (I am thinking of Heidegger in particular) not only is there no acceptance or tolerance of a writing
that had previously been rejected or judged intolerable, but
Plato's distinction is essentially reaffirmed. This is nothing
new: one can find in Heidegger, at least in principle, a kind of
division between *hypomnēsis* and *anamnēsis*, with technique
and writing on one side and poetic thinking on the other –
in short, a bad and a good writing. Perhaps in Nietzsche too,
albeit in a different way.

Once again, then (when raising a question such as writing, for example), one can no longer rely on there being

established passages between the deconstructed tradition and a deconstructive gesture. This is why everything is out of joint, why everything has become disordered and there is no longer any order of time. Texts become so heterogeneous, so little contemporary to themselves, that – in Heidegger, for example – I can find motifs that are radically deconstructive with respect to the classical canon, side by side with gestures that repeat the classical philosophemes in the most faithful, redundant, repetitive and static way imaginable.

Thus the limit always moves within the corpus. If deconstruction is possible, this is because it mistrusts any sort of periodization and moves, or makes its gestures, lines and divisions move, not only within the corpus in general, but at times within a single sentence, or a microscopic element of a corpus. Deconstruction mistrusts proper names: it will not say 'Heidegger in general' says thus or so; it will deal, in the micrology of the Heideggerian text, with different moments, different applications, concurrent logics, while trusting no generality and no configuration that is solid and given. It is a sort of great earthquake, a general tremor, which nothing can calm. I cannot treat a corpus, or a book, as a coherent whole, and even the simple statement is subject to fission. At bottom, this is perhaps what writing is.

I agree with what you said about repressive tolerance. There is an attitude that consists in saying: we accept the philosophers' emancipation from the care for truth and their acceding to literature, their treating philosophy as literature. We won't repress them, we won't denounce them, we won't make fun of them as many academic philosophers do – on the contrary, we'll tolerate them! This gesture, which may seem to be liberal and accommodating, is in fact repressive, insofar as it seeks to strip anyone who complicates the question of philosophy and the relations between philosophy and literature of any claim to deal with truth: to strip them, less of the claim to say what is true, than of the claim be involved with truth. In short, they want to confront us with the following dilemma: 'We'll grant you the right to treat philosophy as literature, but you have to forget this business of claiming to be occupied with truth.'

Now, a moment ago I tried to suggest that the question of truth is not outmoded. Truth is not a value one can renounce. The deconstruction of philosophy does not renounce truth – any more, for that matter, than literature does. It is a question of thinking this other relation to truth. This is not easy, but one must not be intimidated by traditional philosophers (for whom any putting into question of truth is nothing less than an abdication of philosophy, and who denounce the 'non-philosophers' that treat philosophy as literature), nor by that 'repressive tolerance' which consists in accepting one's doing literature, provided that one has no relation with philosophy, with truth, or even, in the extreme, with public space. Someone like Rorty is perfectly happy that we should give ourselves over to literature – on the understanding that it is a private matter, a private language, and that taking shelter in a private language is just fine. I have tried to emphasize the fact that deconstruction has nothing whatsoever to do with privatizing philosophy, letting it take shelter in literature; the gesture, the division, is completely different.

This explains why I would hesitate, for example, to speak of 'post-philosophy'. I find the expression dangerous in any case: there is no simple 'after' philosophy, just as there is no contemporaneity, nor any simple transition to a non-philosophical discourse that would leave philosophy behind. Unless the content one wished to give to the concept of post-philosophy were rigorously specified, I would hesitate to use the term.

I would be even more cautious in responding to what you said about the difference that, as you see it, remains between philosophy and literature. You suggested that what is philosophical proposes, or imposes, itself as that which can survive the difference between languages, crossing over it: a sense, then, is philosophical when it can be translated with nothing lost, while a literary work has so intrinsic, originary and essential a bond with a natural language that there is ultimately no way of translating it. Sure, we do translate literature, but something, you say, is destined to resist the translation; while in that which we call philosophy, what is essential is destined to let itself be translated, and even to make translation possible – which comes down to saying that whatever translation there is in literature is philosophical, and whatever remains untranslatable is more properly literary.

Yes, things do *appear* to look that way. But if it were really the case, then we would be dealing with two different fields, disciplines, texts or events, with philosophy on one side and literature on the other. Without mixing them up, and without reducing the one to the other, perhaps it may be said that *there is always*, in what we call 'philosophical', an adherence to natural language, a profound indissociability of certain philosophemes from the Greek, the German, the Latin, which is not the literary part of philosophy, but is instead something that philosophy shares with literature. And conversely, there is something translatable in literature, a promise of translation, and thus an aspect that is not extraneous to philosophy. Both philosophy and literature are bound up with natural languages: no philosophy exists that may be absolutely formalized in a reduction to a conventional or technical language. Descartes and Leibniz had their dreams, of course, but in fact the reduction is impossible, and for reasons that are not merely factual or empirical. Like literature, philosophy too is indissociably linked to idiom, to the corpora of natural languages. From this point of view, therefore, one cannot speak of language or the relation with language as a border between philosophy and literature.

Yet if the border between them is not constituted by the question of translation, one must still continue to search for their distinctive criteria in the relation with natural language – for philosophy and literature are in fact not the same thing, and it is in this relation that the distinction lies. Both philosophy and literature are composed of works, and these works are bound up with natural languages; the bond, however, like the untranslatability, is not identical in the two cases. Another criterion is needed, and the search for this criterion can and must destroy the great ensembles that give us Plato, Descartes, Kant, Hegel on one side, and Homer, Shakespeare, Goethe on the other; the relation to language is different in *each* case. From the standpoint of language and translation, Plato cannot be treated like Kant, or Leibniz like Hegel, nor can Shakespeare or Dante be treated like Diderot. There are subdivisions that must be kept in mind. This does not stop us, of course, from recognizing the great resemblances that, in spite of everything, give us Plato and Kant on the same side, and Dante and Shakespeare on another. But if we look more closely, we shall find a Platonic literature that is not the literature of Hegel, and a Shakespearean philosophy that is not the philosophy of Dante, Goethe or Diderot. What we have, then, is an enormous research programme, in which the received – or receivable – categories of academic scholarship must not be trusted.

Ferraris.   You have often spoken of strategies (in 'The Ends of Man' [in *Margins of Philosophy*] you even speak of 'pari stratégique' [strategic wager], *à la* Pascal), as if there were a *polemos*.

Derrida.   Of course, if there is *polemos*, and irreducible *polemos*, this cannot, in the final analysis, be accounted for by a taste for war, and still less for polemics. There is *polemos* when a field is determined as a field of battle because there is no metalanguage, no locus of truth outside the field, no absolute and ahistorical overhang; and this absence of overhang – in other words, the radical historicity of the field – makes the field necessarily subject to multiplicity and heterogeneity. As a result, those who are inscribed in this field are necessarily inscribed in a *polemos*, even if they have no special taste for war. There is a strategic destiny, destined to stratagem by the question raised over the truth of the field.

To be sure, speaking of strategy means taking into account an irreducible 'now'. But taking the singularity of this 'now' into account does not force us to renounce what we said earlier about disjunction and the untimely. There is a 'now' of the untimely; there is a singularity which is that of this disjunction of the present.

Formalizing very quickly, I would say, as I have often done in recent years, that the dissociation that imposes itself is a dissociation between the singularity of the 'now' and that of the present. There is 'now' without present; there is singularity of the here and now, even though presence, and self-presence, is dislocated. There are instances of dislocation that are singular, irreplaceable. It is here that the question of what is commonly called 'biography' comes into play: singular existence, even if it is given over to non-self-presence, dislocation, and the non-reappropriation of a present, is for all that no less singular. And so we have to take into account this singularity of the untimely, of non-self-contemporaneity. But precisely because there are none but singular contexts, I shall insist on the question of wager and strategy. If a strategy were guaranteed in and of itself, if its calculation were sure, there would be no strategy at all. Strategy always implies a wager – that is, a certain way of giving ourselves over to not-knowing, to the incalculable. We calculate because there is something incalculable. We calculate where we do not know, where we can make no determination. Thus, a strategic wager always consists in making a decision, or rather in giving ourselves over to the decision – paradoxically, in making decisions we cannot justify from start to finish. The decision to wager is what it is precisely because we do not know whether, at the end of the day, the *pari stratégique* will prove to be the right one, the best one possible. If this were known from the start, there would be no wager, and there would be no strategy. There is a strategic wager because the context is not absolutely determinable: there is a context, but one cannot analyse it exhaustively; the context is open because 'it comes' [*ça vient*], because there is something to come [*il y a de l'avenir*]. We have to accept the concept of a non-saturable context, and take into account both the context itself and its open structure, its non-closure, if we are to make decisions and engage in a wager – or give as a pledge – without knowing, without being sure that it will pay off, that it will be a winner, etc. And this combination of exacerbated responsibility and the acceptance of a part of shadow, of irresponsibility, means that the concern for non-systematic coherence I spoke of at the very beginning leads us to bet on a future [*un avenir*] that would at best reinforce incoherence.

For the moment, to describe this event I shall have to use the old concepts of *oeuvre* and *signature*. *Oeuvre*, because the strategic wager I make at a certain point, when I say 'this rather than that', means that, beyond the limits of this context, tomorrow, whatever the situation may be, what I say will still have a certain consistency – even if there is no scientific value that is omnitemporal and universal, what I say will still be considered an *oeuvre*. So by *oeuvre* I mean something that remains, that is absolutely not translatable, that bears a signature (the signature is not necessarily the narcissism of the proper name or the reappropriation of something that belongs to me); in any case, something that has a place, that has a certain consistency, that is recorded, to which one can return, that can be repeated in a different context, that can be read in the future in a context where reading conditions have changed.

Such a thing will continue to be legible as a certain corpus, with an insistent signature – with a signature that remains the same. A contract is not the proper name, the copyright, the property, but an insistence of the 'same' who signs, who seals the wager. For example, to speak more trivially and concretely, it is clear that, when I began to write such and such about, say, Husserl, the writing corresponded to a context that can be described: a world-wide philosophical context, and more specifically a French context at a certain moment and, even more specifically, in a certain academic field, and so forth. But, over time, the coherence and consistency of what I have called an *oeuvre* should make it possible that – and this is the wager – twenty, thirty, forty years from now what has been said in the context might not simply be contradicted or out of date, and thus might resist – insist – to the point where the context would no longer simply be a collection of conditions circumscribing what I say, but also formed by what I have said within it. In short, when faced with a context it is a question of performatively producing not, of course, a general context, but rather *a certain* context, which neither preceded nor circumscribed its statements, but on the contrary is marked by them. In other words, it is not a question of registering a context but rather of reflecting its outlines, of giving oneself a context and making a mark on it.

What I have called *oeuvre*, making use of this somewhat suspicious or conventional term, is a manner (endogenous, to some degree) of producing the conditions of legibility of that which has been produced. An *oeuvre* is, to a certain extent, its context – not, however, in the sense of autonomy, spontaneous generation and the like, but rather in the sense that one can no longer think the general context without taking the event in question into account. Without making exaggerated or brazen comparisons, let's say that *oeuvres*, be they philosophical or not, are as contextualizing as they are contextualized. One cannot read Plato's time without Plato; which does not mean that Plato fell from the sky, but rather that one must make use of Plato in order to read his time.

Ferraris. Last year, speaking about the attack on Judge Giovanni Falcone, you told me you had the impression that, to a certain degree, Falcone had sought out that destiny. Listening to you, I thought your remark sounded like a projection or an identification. Of you too it can be said, when people accuse you of 'obscurant terrorism', that 'he had it coming', even if this seems unjust and surprising for a philosopher who has always worked well within the canon, and in perfectly legitimate institutions to boot.

Derrida. When someone, driven by a desire that is no doubt obscure, but that we can always try to interpret, says untimely things, or attempts to privilege the untimely, that person is not seeking an absolute untimeliness – which, in any case, he would not find, even if he sought it. There is not that which is in conformity with time on one hand, and that which is absolutely unreceivable in time on the other. Each and every time, epoch, context, culture, each and every national, historical or disciplinary moment, has a certain coherence, but also a certain heterogeneity – it is a system in which there are zones of greater and of lesser receivability. And whoever seeks the untimely attempts to recognize a certain receivability in zones of lesser receivability or conformity. I analyse in a context something that I feel is going against the current, but there is another current, as yet secondary, virtual, inhibited – it waits, pregnant with a possible receivability.

It is a matter of looking for something that is not yet well received, but that waits to be received. And one may possess a kind of flair for that which, going against the current, is already in touch with a possible reception. So – if I may refer to my own case – in all likelihood, each time I have attempted to make a gesture that was, as you said, bizarre or untimely, it was because I had the impression that it was demanded, more or less silently, by other areas of the field, by other forces, that were still in the minority, but that were there. So there is a sort of calculation in the incalculable here, and the untimeliness is a sort of timeliness still in the making.

More often than not it is the most untranslatable texts that are the most translated – these are the works that produce the protocols of translation. This is as true of poetry as it is of philosophy. A work that appears to defy translation is at the same time an appeal for translation; it produces translators, and new protocols of translation; it produces other events that make it possible for a translation that does not exist to be produced. If, once again, I may take my own work as an example, there's no doubt that it is closely linked to the French language; indeed, it has often been accused of multiplying the plays on words, the neologisms, the linguistic oddities linked to an idiom – and so, for this reason, of being all the more untranslatable. But all this has not discouraged translation, and often has made it possible to produce translations that were themselves, in their own languages, events of thought or textual events. What we said about the translation of context is also true of the production of translation.

I would not compare myself with Giovanni Falcone in any way, especially in consideration of the risks he took. But Judge Falcone is a figure of the just man who, in the name of justice, defied the context, the state of the forces. The demands of justice lead a man to defy a context in order to transform it, but here he runs the risk of an incommensurability between his defiance and the state of the forces; this is the absolute risk. Falcone bore witness for justice at the risk of his own life, while taking account of the context (he knew it better than anyone else); but at a given moment he did not yield to the dissuasion exercised by that context, he did not abdicate before the demand of justice. And here, what I have called 'justice', which is not the same as 'right' or 'law' [*droit*], is a relation to the unconditional that, once all the conditional givens have been taken into account, bears witness to that which will not allow itself to be enclosed within a context.[1] It is clear that this relation to the unconditional – to justice – is a matter of life and death. Justice is not right [*droit*]; it is that which attempts, nonetheless, to produce a new right. And to do so it is necessary, first, to take the context into account and then, at a given moment, to transform it radically.

You are surprised at the fact that certain people refuse to recognize someone as a philosopher when he has dedicated himself to the great philosophers of the canon, and has taught in institutions of higher learning that are apparently quite legitimate. But if you take a closer look you will find, first, that the way in which I have dedicated myself to these canonical philosophers has, naturally, not altogether conformed to the usual treatment of this canon; and second, that the academic institutions that have hosted and even 'crowned' me, so to speak, were themselves marginal – prestigious yes, but not universities. You have to keep in mind that I did teach in major institutions, but during a time when entrance to the university was refused me. A closer look at the field of higher education in France would make it clear that – not only in my own case – installing someone in a major institution may be precisely a way of rejecting him, or a confirmation of his rejection on other institutional levels. This would get us involved in the history of

---

[1] *Droit* may be translated into English as either 'right' or 'law'. In expressions such as 'the right [*droit*] to remain silent' [pp. 25–6 below], the choice is unproblematic. However, where *droit* is opposed to *justice*, as in the present case (and other similar cases below), the decision is less clear: as when translating the German *Recht*, 'law' tends to be too restrictive, and 'right' perhaps too broad. 'Law' also corresponds to *loi*, *Gesetz* and the Latin *lex*, which is opposed to *droit*, *Recht*, *ius*. In the text, *droit* will be translated as 'right' or 'law' as English idiom demands [Eds].

the French institutions – the relation between the university, the Ecole Normale, the Collège de France, the Hautes Etudes; all this is not an opposition between the legitimate and the illegitimate, but rather a very complicated distribution of the demands of legitimacy.

Paris, 16 July 1993

II

Justice without strength is powerless. Strength without justice is tyrannical. Justice without strength is a contradiction
because there are always wicked people. Strength without
justice is an indictment. So justice and strength must be joined,
and for that, what is just must be made strong, or what is
strong, just.

> Pascal, *Pensées*, trans. Honor Levi, §125, p. 34

Derrida. In dealing with what-is-to-come [*l'avenir*],[2] with
the opening to the to-come [*l'à-venir*] – that is, not only to
the future [*futur*], but to what happens [*ce qui arrive*], comes
[*vient*], has the form of an event – this opening must certainly
be linked up with what we said yesterday about context: with
a movement that consists not only in inscribing itself in a
context – and from this point of view there is nothing but
context – but thereby also in producing a context, transforming a given [*donné*] context, opening it up and bringing
about a new contextual giving [*donne*: hand of cards]. From
this point of view, a work [*oeuvre*] – or, for that matter, a
phrase or a gesture, a mark [*marque*] or a chain of marks –
inflects a context and, in so doing, appeals for a new one. A
simple phrase takes its meaning from a given context, and
already makes its appeal to another one in which it will be

---

[2] Although *avenir* will usually be translated as 'future', Derrida plays throughout
the text on the sense of 'coming' implicit within it; the sense of *à venir*, 'to come'.
A similar sense of movement is expressed by *arriver*, which can mean both to
arrive and to happen [Eds].

understood; but, of course, to be understood it has to transform the context in which it is inscribed. As a result, this
appeal, this promise of the future, will necessarily open up
the production of a new context, wherever it may happen
[*arrive*]. The future *is not present*, but *there is* an opening
onto it; and because *there is* a future [*il y a de l'avenir*], a
context is always open. What we call opening of the context
is another name for what is still to come.

Justice – or justice as it promises to be, beyond what it
actually is – always has an eschatological dimension. I link up
this value of eschatology with a certain value of messianism,
in an attempt to free both dimensions from the *religious* and
philosophical contents and manifestations usually attached
to them: philosophical, for eschatology, the thought of the
extreme, the *eschaton*; or religious, the messianism in the
religions 'of the book'. Why do I claim that justice is eschatological and messianic, and that this is so *a priori*, even for the
non-believer, even for someone who does not live according
to a faith determined by Judeo-Christian-Islamic revelation?
Perhaps because the appeal of the future [*l'avenir*] that we
spoke of a moment ago – which overflows any sort of ontological determination, which overflows everything that is and
that is present, the entire field of being and beings, and the
entire field of history – is committed to a promise or an appeal
that goes beyond being and history. This is an extremity
that is beyond any determinable end of being or of history,
and this eschatology – as extreme beyond the extreme, as
last beyond the last – has necessarily to be the only absolute
opening towards the non-determinability of the future.

It is perhaps necessary to free the value of the future from
the value of 'horizon' that traditionally has been attached to
it – a horizon being, as the Greek word indicates, a limit from
which I pre-comprehend the future. I wait for it, I pre-
determine it, and thus I annul it. Teleology is, at bottom,
the negation of the future, a way of knowing beforehand
the form that will have to be taken by what is still to come.

Here, what I call the eschatological or the messianic is
nothing other than a relation to the future so despoiled and
indeterminate that it leaves being 'to come' [*à venir*], i.e.,

undetermined. As soon as a determinate outline is given to the future, to the promise, even to the Messiah, the messianic loses its purity, and the same is true of the eschatological in the sense we are giving it now. We would find ourselves with a sort of messianic eschatology so desertic that no religion and no ontology could identify themselves with it. If we had the texts on hand, it would be interesting to look at the passages where Heidegger talks about eschatology. In any case, what we have here is an affirmation that is, moreover, a decision, implicit within any relation to the future – a reaffirmation of the eschatological and messianic as a structured relation to the future as such. If there is a future as such, it cannot even announce itself, it cannot be pre-announced or over-announced [se sur-annoncer] except in the eschatological and messianic – but in a messianic and an eschatological that would be the kenosis of the eschatological and messianic. This kenosis does not necessarily have to be the object of a mystical exercise or ascetic despoilment. Nevertheless, we do have to recognize the fact that it works messianically and eschatologically on our present, our 'now', our everydayness. And this 'now' is not a present.

How can the desert of this kenosis be linked to justice? It may be said: 'with a despoilment of this sort, even if it be granted you, you will never render justice to justice; justice has nothing to do with it.' But I do not agree. What has to be 'saved' by this kenosis, if it is the irruption of a future that is absolutely non-reappropriable, has to have the shape of the other, which is not simply the shape of something in space that cannot be reached. That which defies anticipation, reappropriation, calculation – any form of pre-determination – is *singularity*. There can be no future as such unless there is radical otherness, and respect for this radical otherness. It is here – in that which ties together as non-reappropriable the future and radical otherness – that justice, in a sense that is a little enigmatic, analytically participates in the future. Justice has to be thought of as what overflows law [*droit*], which is always an ensemble of determinable norms, positively incarnated and positive. But justice has to be distinguished not only from law, but also from what *is* in general.

I can well imagine the objections raised here by people concerned with law, politics and morals against such a phantom idea of justice – objections that have to be answered. The question of the political, ethical, juridical, consists in finding, as the occasion demands, the schemata required to articulate justice and law, justice and politics, justice and history, justice and ontology. But with all due respect for the enormity of the problems – which are indeed the problems we have to resolve whenever we make a decision or take political action – I think that the instant one loses sight of the *excess* of justice, or of the future, in that very moment the conditions of totalization would, undoubtedly, be fulfilled – but so would the conditions of the *totalitarianism* of a right [*droit*] without justice, of a good moral conscience and a good juridical conscience, which all adds up to a present without a future [*sans avenir*]. I do not want to take sides in a war of religions, but the religions for which the Messiah has arrived, where the messianic vocation has already been accomplished, always run the risk of lacking this transcendence of justice and the to-come with respect to totality.

The same is true as regards the theme – related, but distinct – of recognition, of wishing to be recognized. Here, it is less a question of being recognized for its own sake than of being recognized in a certain way, *not for what one is* but rather for what one would like to be. At this point the problem of recognition is not quite so simple – since the problem of the narcissistic image comes into play. If 'I' wish to be recognized not for what I am at present but rather, for example, for what I try to say about justice – which is to say, for something that overflows all ontological determinations, and my own in particular (what I just said about justice is so excessive with respect to my name that I could not even think of signing or reappropriating it) – this is not in order to be recognized as what I am, but has a completely different purpose. Naturally, I want what I say to be understood. But I cannot wish to be understood in order to reappropriate what I said as my work or to get credit for it. That may happen anyway, it may be part of the bargain, but it's not what is essential. In what I say and what I write, I put this injunction ahead of a great many others (if I were someone who said 'look at me', I wouldn't care much about saying such things). And I don't say this to encourage anyone to make fun of recognition or narcissism; I often try to put the concept of narcissism into question, since it is a very important question that has been poorly defined. There is, however, a point where narcissism opens up, where the specular relation between consciousnesses opens onto something other than itself, and it is this point that must be taken into account. But it cannot be accounted for if this accounting consists in any sort of 'counting', i.e. of calculation – because what we have been speaking of, under the name of the future, justice, the messianic and eschatological, is something *incalculable*. It is the *excess* of justice with respect to the accounted for, to calculable right and accountability – the excess of responsibility with respect to accountability and calculability.

In saying this I wish to be recognized, but what I have said is something that I cannot reappropriate. This is why the eschatological or messianic, even if they have the form of expectation, hope, promise – motifs that are apparently so striking – is also the experience of death. When I say this, I know I am speaking of my death – where, to be sure, I can reappropriate nothing, where I will no longer be able to reappropriate the future. Only a mortal can speak of the future in this sense, a god could never do so. So I know very well that all this is a discourse – an experience, rather – that is made possible as a future by a certain imminence of death. The imminence here is the fact that death may arrive in any moment – Heidegger discusses this brilliantly in *Being and Time* – and the fact that death may arrive in any moment gives this justice the character of an immediate injunction.

I would like to anticipate an objection, which goes like this: since justice is always in excess with respect to right, it can never be attained, is always deferred, and so is not even an infinite idea in the Kantian sense but is even further removed, and is excessive in any case – and therefore one may be excused for not attaining it. But not at all! This excess *presses* urgently here and now, *singularly*. It does not wait. Imminence means that it presses in every instant: *this* is never present, but *this* will not be put off to tomorrow: *this*, the relation to the other – death.

Ferraris. In a famous passage of the *Phenomenology of Spirit*, Hegel opposes virtue in the ancient world – which was rooted in the substance of the people, having a real content as an already existing good, and thus was not directed against actual reality and the 'way of the world' as against something perverted – to a romantic virtue devoid of content, which is virtue in name only, and in its empty rebellion 'signifies nothing'. Hegel goes on to stigmatize this vain chatter – and rightly so, I think, especially in the light of the endless talk about ethics that has become the commonplace of our own time even more than it was of Hegel's. Nevertheless it is true that, following Kierkegaard, the instant of decision is madness; which is to say that a normative ethics meets its absolute limit in the fact that no rule and no content can determine the ultimate demand of a decision. But if this is true there would be no sense in reproposing the dream of an ethics regulated by the contents of an organic community (such as, for example, the ones that restrained Socrates from revolting against the laws of his city); but perhaps it would be appropriate to think that which, in 'Violence and Metaphysics' [in *Writing and Difference*], you called 'community of the question' or of interrogation – a community of interpretation and allegoresis [*allégorèse*].

Derrida.   Clearly, I would be far more at ease speaking of community in this sense – a community of allegoresis, a community that is such only in an alliance that not only does not cancel out the singularity of the allies but, on the contrary, accentuates it. I would have far fewer difficulties and reservations in accepting the image of a community that does not constitute itself on the basis of a contemporaneity of presences but rather through the opening produced by what you have called allegoresis – that is, the interpretation of a text not given, not closed in on itself, an interpretation that itself transforms the text. We would have, then, a community of writing and reading – a community that would be bound by a testament to the law that is neither given in advance nor understood in advance. These Tables of the Law have to exist already – not be present, but already exist – if the future is to remain open to what is still to be done, read and written. I have no misgivings about this community, it's just that there is something that would always make me hesitate to call it 'community' – namely, that the force of the future that has to be at work in it has to be a force of disruption no less than a force of integration, a force of dissension no less than a force of consensus.

Why call it community? Just to conform to what certain of our friends have attempted to do, to Blanchot's 'unavowable' community or Nancy's 'inoperative' one? I have no qualms about these communities; my only question is, why call them communities? If I have always hesitated to use this word, it is because too often the word 'community' resounds with the 'common' [*commun*], the as-one [*comme-un*]. But, as long as one takes the precautions you indicated, I have no objections, for I know perfectly well that disruption in itself is not sufficient, that disparity and dissension cannot be sufficient to respond to justice; and it's also clear that justice, the messianic, the relation to the other, cannot be identified with anti-community. But when Blanchot himself, for example, affirms both the 'unavowable community' and that the relation to the other has to be an interruption, then we have a community that does right by interruption! The word 'community' bothers me only because of certain connotations it too often retains, even in 'communism' as Blanchot defines it in certain passages of *Friendship* or *The Infinite Conversation*. This is a communism where the common is anything but common; it is the placing in common [*mise en commun*] of that which is no longer of the order of subjectivities, or of intersubjectivity as a relation – however paradoxical – between presences. Everything we have been saying here is a certain way of questioning community in the classical sense, and intersubjectivity as well.

Ferraris. While the right to remain silent – to refuse to answer – is formally granted by a court of justice, this is not the case in the media and literary court, where moreover the existence of a right to reply can be highly dubious at times. So it is not so much a question of looking for community, since in a certain sense community already exists too much, in the form, both trivial and massive, of the family, of all families. You have often cited Gide's indictment of the family, adding to it your own private translation: 'I am not one of the family' [*je ne suis pas de la famille*].

Derrida.   Before coming to that saying of mine, I would like to say a few words about the right to remain silent, to refuse to answer. The glaring paradox here is that, on one hand, democracy, especially in the form it wants to give to freedom of expression, the press and opinion, ought to guarantee the right to reply. But, on the other, our everyday experience tells us it does not do so, and in fact does so less all the time, with the development of mass media and their one-sided communication; even if the law (in France in particular) accords a right to reply, one knows that this right is never technically ensured. As a result democracy is never ensured and never will be – will never be what it has to be, unless this right is absolutely guaranteed.

And it never will be. This is one phase of the question: the lack of a right to reply in democracy. If democracy is always 'to come', this is because the right to reply, which is an infinite right, will never be fully ensured. This can be easily demonstrated.

Taking the question the other way around, the self-same concept of democracy is founded on subjective responsibility, i.e. on the subject's obligation to answer. And thus on the fact that he has no right not to answer. In a democracy, when someone asks you your name you have to answer; public space is a space in which a subject is questioned and has to answer. If someone who is called upon to testify, vote, give his name, replies 'I'm not answering', 'I refuse to answer', he can be put in prison. Although democracy ought to guarantee both the right to answer and the right not to answer, in fact it guarantees neither the one nor the other. One of my favourite literary paradigms is 'Bartleby the Scrivener', who neither answers nor doesn't answer when he says 'I would prefer not to'. He doesn't say no and he doesn't say yes. There's a great deal to be said about this immense text of Melville's. And there is something analogous in Dickens, where we find a relation to the other in which I say neither yes nor no, I say: 'I don't want the freedom to rebel, revolt or refuse, I want the freedom not to answer, to sign statements that say neither yes nor no, and a neither yes nor no that isn't simply a double negation or a dialectic. "I would prefer not to." That this figure is linked to death – well, there's a great deal to be said about this, about the question of not answering as a fundamental political question.

That said, let me get back to my saying 'I am not one of the family'. Clearly, I was playing on a formula that has multiple registers of resonance. I'm not one of the family means, in general 'I do not define myself on the basis of my belonging to the family', or to civil society, or to the state; I do not define myself on the basis of elementary forms of kinship. But it also means, more figuratively, that I am not part of any group, that I do not identify myself with a linguistic community, a national community, a political party, or with any group or clique whatsoever, with any philosophical or literary school. 'I am not one of the family' means: do not consider me 'one of you', 'don't count me in', I want to keep my freedom, always: this, for me, is the condition not only for being singular and other, but also for entering into relation with the singularity and alterity of others. When someone is one of the family, not only does he lose himself in the herd, but he loses the others as well; the others become simply places, family functions, or places or functions in the organic totality that constitutes a group, school, nation or community of subjects speaking the same language.

This quip also reflects a sort of idiosyncrasy of my own, stemming from my highly unusual family history. The fact is that I have a predisposition to not being one of the family, it wasn't just my choice. I am a Jew from Algeria, from a certain type of community, in which belonging to Judaism was problematic, belonging to Algeria was problematic, belonging to France was problematic, etc. So all this predisposed me to not-belonging; but, beyond the particular idiosyncrasies of my own story, I wanted to indicate the sense in which an 'I' does not have to be 'one of the family'.

But then, if we want to look at this statement in another light, the saying 'I am not one of the family' does not simply describe a fact, or way of being. Although I have treated it this way, it can also mean: 'I do not want to be one of the family'. 'I am not one of the family' is a performative, a commitment. Once we have distinguished the performative from a description, we can go on to analyse it. The first dimension of the performative is what I have just said: I am not one of the family, 'don't count me in'. But the second dimension, which in a sense is lodged in the first, and which overflows it, is that the fact of my *not wanting* to be one of the family is *supposed* by the fact of *wanting* to be one of the family. The desire to belong to any community whatsoever, the desire for belonging *tout court*, implies that one *does not belong*. I could not say 'I want to be one of the family' if in fact I *was* one of the family. To put it another way, I could not say 'I want to be Italian, European, to speak this language, etc.', if that were already the case. *Accounting for one's belonging* – be it on national, linguistic, political or philosophical grounds – in itself implies a not-belonging. This can have political consequences: there is no identity. There is identification, belonging is accounted for, but this itself implies that the belonging does not exist, that the people who want to be this or that – French, European, etc. – are *not so* in fact. And they have to know this! This is why the family is something to which one never belongs, to which one always belongs – which is why the family is something so dramatic, because the family (the nation, humanity) has no self-identity. It is never a state.

Ferraris.   According to Aristotle, a man is father of his books as he is of his children. A certain image or anticipation of maturity leads one, at a certain age, to project an idealized image of a work. Let's take as an example the age of 37 – the age at which Hegel published the *Phenomenology of Spirit*, Heidegger *Being and Time*, and you *Writing and Difference*, *Speech and Phenomena*, *Of Grammatology*.

Derrida. Indecent analogies! How tempted I am to interpret all these consonances and harmonies – what links familial paternity to the paternity of a work, and what takes its place in an optimum maturation, at a certain age – in other words, all this teleology assumed in your synopsis! But I am also tempted by the opposite – I'm tempted to show that it is because paternity is impossible that the relation to a work is not a relation of paternity, and thus that there is always an inadequacy in the very idea of paternity: that one can sign neither a child nor a work. Being a father means having the extremely joyful and painful experience of the fact that one is not the father – that a son or daughter is someone one does not answer for, or who answers for themselves, who can speak for themselves. And thus paternity is neither a state nor a property – be it in the sense of family filiation or in the sense of the filiation of what we call a text or a work. This inadequacy of propriety [*propriété*: property, ownership] to itself, this impropriety [*impropriété*] presses forward, it makes one continue. If someone who is in the process of having children, or of signing a work or a phrase, does not stop, it is precisely because she knows that it goes on after her and is essentially non-coincident with and non-adequate to her. So it is rather a logic of dislocation, a-teleology, non-completeness, that I see in this trajectory.

As for the question of what can occur, say, at the age of 37, you have improperly and generously compared me to great philosophers who signed great works at that age. But as it happens what I published at thirty-seven was anything but a great matrix work. What I wrote were articles, not books; it was all a sort of confluence of small texts, none of which on its own was sufficient to make up a book. It would be easy to show how none of those volumes, be it *Of Grammatology*, *Writing and Difference* or *Speech and Phenomena* – not one of them is a book, not one of them was planned as a book. I can show this in a few words: *Writing and Difference* is a collection of texts, dating from 1962–3 to 1967; *Of Grammatology* is made up of two heterogeneous passages put together somewhat artificially (the first part and the part on Rousseau), and this logic of supplementarity is a logic of incompleteness; as for *Speech and Phenomena*, that was a conference presentation, I wrote it in a few weeks in the summer for a conference in the United States, and then I showed it to Hyppolite who said to me 'it could be made into a book' – that's how it happened, but it was anything but a project for a book. So none of this looks like a blossoming or a completeness, but rather like impromptus, fits and starts that, precisely because of their incompleteness and the non-coincidence I mentioned a moment ago, induced me to continue – yes, in part because I wanted to prevent misunderstandings, to be more specific, but also in order to prolong the non-coincidence.

Ferraris. But it would be easy to object that Hegel or Heidegger might have said the same thing and to turn your discourse upside down, showing for instance that what you are saying is precisely what Rousseau said to justify all his work. As he put it, it is not a question of writing books, but rather of rectifying misunderstandings stemming from the first unfortunate time that one ventured to publish something. And then, with regard to the question of preventing misunderstandings, this implies that one wishes to be understood (which is the argument Gadamer produces to counter your thesis that the ultimate *telos* of communication does not consist in understanding).

Derrida. Here, I am tempted to say that my own experience of writing leads me to think that one does not always write with a desire to be understood – that there is a paradoxical desire not to be understood. It's not simple, but there is a certain 'I hope that not everyone understands everything about this text', because if such a transparency of intelligibility were ensured it would destroy the text, it would show that the text has no future [*avenir*], that it does not overflow the present, that it is consumed immediately. Consequently a certain zone of disacquaintance, of not-understanding, is also a reserve and an excessive chance – a chance for excess to have a future, and consequently to engender new contexts. If everyone can understand immediately what I mean to say – all the world all at once – then I have created no context,

I have mechanically fulfilled an expectation, and then it's over, even if people applaud and read with pleasure; for then they close the book and it's all over.

Thus there is the desire, which may appear a bit perverse, to write things that not everyone will be able to appropriate through immediate understanding. I have often been accused of writing things that are unnecessarily difficult, that could be simplified, and I have even been accused of doing it on purpose. I'd say that this accusation is just and unjust at the same time. It is unjust because I really do try to be clear; it's not that I amuse myself multiplying obstacles to understanding; I can even be pedagogical – often *too* pedagogical, perhaps. But I have to admit that there is a demand in my writing for this excess even with respect to what I myself can understand of what I say – the demand that a sort of opening, play, indetermination be left, signifying hospitality for what is to come [*l'avenir*]: 'One does not know what it means yet, one will have to start again, to return, to go on.' And if there were time, it could be shown precisely how each text enacts a kind of opening – as the Bible puts it – of the place left vacant for who is to come [*pour qui va venir*], for the *arrivant* – maybe Elijah, maybe anyone at all. There has to be the possibility of someone's still arriving; there has to be an *arrivant*, and consequently the table – the table of contents or the table of the community – has to mark an empty place for someone absolutely indeterminate, for an *arrivant* – who may be called the Messiah, but that's another question. And there, where there is place for the *arrivant*, the text is not intelligible, the discourse bears a zone of emptiness that, moreover, has a great deal to do with what we said earlier about kenosis.

But this is also a way of giving to be read [donner à lire]. If something is given to be read that is totally intelligible, that can be totally saturated by sense, it is not given to the other to be read. Giving to the other to be read is also a *leaving to be desired*, or a leaving the other room for an intervention by which she will be able to write her own interpretation: the other will have to be able to sign in my text. And it is here that the desire not to be understood means, simply, hospitableness to the reading of the other, not the rejection of the other.

Ferraris.   In your 1954 dissertation, *Le problème de la genèse dans la philosophie de Husserl*, you recalled *Faith and Knowledge*: experience and the a priori, far from being opposed, are the same, because phenomenal experience of the real is a synthesis a priori. The trace of the past is also a trace of the future, an empirical function proves to be transcendental, because the very temporality on the basis of which a priori and a posteriori are divided is itself produced in experience. In other words, the Hegelian dialectic itself demonstrates that there is no justification for stigmatizing in *The Critique of Pure Reason* a 'consecration of the finite' in the style of the Enlightenment and of Locke, as Hegel himself does in *Faith and Knowledge*.

Derrida.   You refer to the pair transcendental-dialectical. If we take, for example, that which makes a dialectical process possible – namely, an element foreign to the system that transcends a group of categories (the transcendental as that which *transcendit omne genus*), an element more or less than a table or series of categories – this foreign element, more originary than the dialectic, is precisely that which the dialectic is to dialectize, taking it into and including it in itself. This is why the most dialectical formulations of the dialectic, those which in general are to be found in Hegel, are always both dialectical and non-dialectical: identity of non-identity and identity. The non-dialectical does not oppose the dialectical, and is a figure that recurs continually. I have constantly attempted to single out that element which would not allow itself to be integrated in a series or a group, in order to show that *there is* a non-oppositional difference that transcends the dialectic, which is itself always oppositional. There is a supplement, or a *pharmakon* – I could give many more examples – that does not let itself be dialectized. Precisely that which, not being dialectical, makes dialectic impossible, is necessarily retaken by the dialectic that it relaunches. At this point, we have to remark that the dialectic consists precisely in dialectizing the non-dialectizable. What we have, then, is a concept of dialectic that is no longer the conventional one of synthesis, conciliation, reconciliation, totalization, identification with itself; now, on the contrary, we have a negative or an infinite dialectic that is the movement of synthesizing without synthesis. It is, for example, what I call *ex-appropriation*, which is in principle an anti-dialectical concept; but it can always be interpreted as the *nec plus ultra* of the dialectical, as in *Le problème de la genèse*.

And this is why, after that highly dialectizing first book of mine, whenever I insisted on a non-dialectizable difference, I remarked with discretion, but markedly, that it was not a question of opposing a dialectic. I have never *opposed* the dialectic. Be it opposition to the dialectic or war against the dialectic, it's a losing battle. What it really comes down to is thinking a dialecticity of dialectics that is itself fundamentally not dialectical.

What I've said here about the dialectic is also true of *dialegesthai*, dialogue, intelligibility, justice, etc.; but, basically, we are dealing with two concepts or two figures of the dialectic – the conventional one, of totalization, reconciliation and reappropriation through the work of the negative etc.; and then a non-conventional figure, which I have just indicated. Clearly, between the two figures themselves there will also have to be a dialectic – in this case, between the non-dialectizable and the dialectizable. And the *non* of the non-dialectizable itself splits in two: it may be thought as a *non* of opposition or as a *non* of irreducibility, of heterogeneity. Thus the non-dialectizable may be apprehended as dialectical or non-dialectical, as oppositional or heterogeneous.

What has always worried me is the heterogeneous, namely, *that which does not even oppose*: it may be called either the greatest *force of opposition* to dialectic, or the greatest *weakness*. I have often felt that the image of weakness offers less purchase to dialectic. It is the weak, not the strong, that defies dialectic. Right is dialectical, justice is not dialectical, justice is weak. Nietzsche in particular saw and understood better than others the process of conversion by which the greatest weakness becomes the greatest strength. Is it a dialectical proposition that the greatest weakness – philosophy, Christianity – prevailed over the greatest strength, and that this perversion is morality, the origin of debt and guilt, etc.? Is it a dialectical proposition or not, when Nietzsche says that dialectic is the victory of the weak, but is at the same time a manifestation of strength? I do not know whether this movement can be called 'dialectical'. Nietzsche, of course, would deny it – but wasn't he himself being dialectical when he said it?

Is the given dialectizable? If that was the gist of your question, I think that, in a Hegelian sense, yes, the dialectic begins here: for something to be determined in intuition, the first determination of the this and the here-and-now is the absolutely incompressible, unarrestable beginning of the autonomous movement of the dialectic. The given is dialectical. But, clearly, one can rightly think the gift [*don*] of the given [*donné*] as that which simultaneously precedes the dialectic and interrupts it. That is what I try to say about the gift in *Given Time*: the gift is precisely what must not present itself. In this sense it is never given, it must not be given as something, nor by someone. Whatever there is of gift in the given [*de don dans le donné*], it is not a given. Understood in this sense, or thought, or promised, the given is truly the non-dialectizable: it is what resists economy, circulation – it is what resists the circle. It can always be demonstrated that as soon as one attempts to say what one means by 'gift', to determine or speak of it, one is in the dialectic. But here it is a question of thinking a thing that is not a thing, and that under the name of 'gift' can be neither known nor made phenomenal. The phenomenalization of the gift annuls the gift, and thus there is no phenomenality here, no phenomenology, no ontology (the gift is not a 'present' – i.e. a present being). In defying ontology and phenomenology, the gift defies the dialectic. It is a gift that ought to have nothing to do with what is called the 'given' in philosophy – with what is present, what is here, and that temporal or spatial intuition can receive as a content or phenomenon.

Ris-Orangis, 17 July 1993

III

A race eager to know about another man's life, but slothful
to correct their own! Why do they seek to hear from me what
I am, men who do not want to hear from you what they
themselves are? When they hear me speak about myself,
how do they know if I speak the truth, since none among
men knows 'what goes on within a man but the spirit of
man which is in him'?

The Confessions of St Augustine, X, 3.3, trans.
John K. Ryan, p. 230

Derrida. If Nietzsche has always been such an important
point of reference for me – I still remember the first time I
read him, in Algeria – this is first of all because he is a
thinker who practises a *psychology of philosophers*. Great
philosophers, he often said, are produced by a certain psychology, a certain history of the *psychē*, which is clearly
not the history of a *Weltanschauung* in Dilthey's sense, nor
is it a historical psychology, one regional discipline among
others. Philosophy is psychology and biography together, a
movement of the living *psychē*, and thus of individual life
and the strategy of this life, insofar as it assembles all the
philosophemes and all the ruses of truth.

In my own history, I have always had to reconcile this motif,
which I still set great store by, with a basically Husserlian one,
namely the critique of psychologism – the break with that
element of psychology which runs the risk of contradicting
or making impossible the scientific project or the philosophic
project as such. For me, the critique of psychologism was an

important matter; I took it very seriously. It was an essential
philosophical lever. In this logic of the critique of psychologism, I recall how interested I was in Husserl's idea (in fact
I wrote about it in 1963, in a review of his *Phenomenological
Psychology*) that between pure phenomenological psychology,
transcendental psychology, on the one hand, and pure transcendental phenomenology of the ego on the other, there
is no *real difference*, once all the reductions have been performed. There are *parallels*. There is a parallel or coincidence
between the contents of pure phenomenological psychology
(which remains a science of the *psychē*, i.e. of a region of
the world, and of the region on the basis of which the world
is organized) and constitutive transcendental phenomenology
(the *Ur-Region* of transcendental consciousness, which is not
in the world). *Nothing* separates them, no content distinguishes them. But there is *a nothing* between them that does
not appear as such, and which is decisive. It is the question
of this *nothing* that has always interested me. I have always
situated myself, more or less comfortably, happily or uneasily,
on the line or limit between the irreducibility of the psychological and psychoanalytical, and a thought that is philosophical
or deconstructive of philosophy, where philosophy implies
independence of the psychical, or at least of that psychical
which is the object of a science called 'psychology'. This, for
me, has always been the locus of the problem. It is also the
locus in which the question of the signature, psychology and
intellectual autobiography is posed: *Who* thinks? *Who* signs?
What do we make of *singularity* in this experience of thought?
And what do we make of the relation between life, death
and *psychē*?

Ferraris. 1942. 'France now, the French university. You
accuse me of being pitiless, and above all unjust with it (scores
to be settled perhaps: did they not expel me from school
when I was 11, no German having set foot in Algeria? The
only school official whose name I remember today: he has
me come into his office: "You are going to go home, my
little friend, your parents will get a note." At the moment
I understood nothing, but since? Would they not start all

over, if they could, prohibiting me from school? Is it not for this reason that I have for ever ensconced myself in it in order to provoke them to it and to give them the most urgent wish, always at the limit, to expel me again? No, I do not at all, but not at all, believe these hypotheses, they are seductive or amusing, manipulable, but without value, they are clichés. And then you know that I am not for the destruction of the universitas or the disappearance of the guardians, but precisely one has to make a certain war against them when obscurantism, vulgarity above all, becomes ensconced, as is inevitable.' (J. Derrida, *The Post Card*, trans. Alan Bass, pp. 87–8)

Derrida.   The date you have chosen, 1942, for me denotes a fracture or a trauma. An unconscious sedimentation formed, hardened in me at that time, but also, no less unconsciously, an intellectual determination – even if I didn't understand much about what was going on in 1942, when I, the little Jew from Algiers, with the onset of anti-Semitism (French, not Nazi, anti-Semitism) was expelled from school. Even though I understood very little, through that wound there was ensconced in me a certain conscious–unconscious way of looking at intellectual matters – at culture and the language problem. Albeit unconsciously, a configuration that later on would come to be called intellectual, and even ideological, had already taken shape. From that point on, it is no longer possible – for me or for anybody else – to distinguish the biographical from the intellectual, the non-intellectual from the intellectual biography, the conscious from the unconscious. To give a rigorous and discerning description of these sequences, to really do something more than just tell stories (more or less spectacular anecdotes) about what went on at that time, it would be necessary to find new categories, to invent an extremely refined instrument that is diegetical, phenomenological and psychoanalytical all at the same time.

If I use current, immediately available language, what is there for me to say about the intellectual aspect of my story? Here we have a 12-year-old boy who, without anyone explaining to him what anti-Semitism is, or what is happening politically, is kicked out of school one day by a *surveillant général* who tells him 'you are going to go home, you parents will explain it to you'. A crack is opened in the relative security represented by the school, the place where culture is offered him, where languages are taught – especially the dominant models of the French language.

French is the only mother tongue I have, but while still a child I had a vague sensation that this language was not really my own. This was not just because I belonged to a Jewish family, of Spanish origin, present in Algeria even before the French colonization, but also because ever since I started school – so here begins my 'intellectual biography' – and from the very beginning the manner in which the French language was taught, the norms of 'proper' speaking and writing, the references to literature, all made it pretty clear that the model was in France – and not just in France, but in Paris. So I had the feeling that this language, which was the only one I had, came from somewhere else. And the time when I was excluded from school must have aggravated my feeling of extraneousness and exteriority, of not belonging. Already in the language, already in the reference to literature, to the model of *bien-parler* and *bien-écrire*. This violent rupture must have left its mark, even if I didn't know what it meant, even if in a certain sense I didn't even protest (to the best of my memory, the day they told me 'go home' I had no feeling of revolt or indignation, just of incomprehension, and I remained in that state of incomprehension, since no one in my family explained to me what was going on). A short time later my parents enrolled me in a Jewish school in Algiers, as most of the Jewish families were doing, where a great many Jewish teachers who had also been kicked out of school ended up teaching French to young Jewish pupils in a Jewish school that was like a *lycée*.

The first few months after my expulsion was a very bad time; I had begun to experience anti-Semitism outside, in the streets, in my circle of friends, my old playmates who treated me like a 'dirty Jew' and wouldn't talk to me any more. And, paradoxically, the feeling of not belonging came to affect my relationship with the Jewish community and with the Jewish children who, like me, had been grouped together in the Jewish school. I hated that school. More often than not, without telling my parents, I just cut classes. I was on very bad terms with the Jewish community, which was trying to get organized and adapt to the situation. In that period an obscure feeling arose in me that has, I think, remained to this day – a trauma that caused me not only to cultivate a sort of not-belonging to French culture and to France in general, but also, in some way, to reject my belonging to Judaism. This, at least, is my impression: in those few months, in 1942–3, certain things jelled and became a permanent part of me. My spontaneous or infantile reaction to anti-Semitic violence consisted in saying 'no, I am part neither of this nor of that', neither of this anti-Semitism nor of its victims – a haughty and affected gesture, without sympathy for the self-protecting attitude of the Jewish community, which tended to close ranks when endangered. I never took part in any group of Jewish students.

Of course, I can attempt a logical, rational description of this double movement, as I have been doing now; but it is probable that these things took place very far from my consciousness, and perhaps they are far from it even now. Of course, I can also rationalize and transform not-belonging into an ethico-political duty, saying that belonging is a non-belonging, and saying that it is on the basis of a non-belonging that faithfulness is constructed. But there is probably a sort of indelible suffering that goes back to that time of my life.

In a certain way, I attempted to speak about this in 1980 in *The Post Card*, as you showed. Later, in 'Circumfession' [in J. Derrida and G. Bennington, *Jacques Derrida*, trans. G. Bennington], justifiably or not, I went all the way back to an experience that took place even before the trauma of which we have just spoken – I am thinking of the distress I felt on my first day at infant school, a terrible moment of tears and anguish that was to be repeated practically every year. So there is effectively a chain of events leading from my first separation from the family milieu to go to school, to the expulsion of 1942, followed by the whole institutional drama – the fact that even though I have always been *in* school I was never good *at* school. I failed a lot of examinations, was held back, and sometimes had to put up with resistance and attempts to marginalize me in the French university, right up to my experience in Prague where I was put in prison, and where the institution took the form of a metal door. Like the door of a school or the door of a prison, that metal door has always been there to indicate a desire for non-belonging, forced belonging, etc.

Ferraris.   1948–9. 'The movement towards philosophy takes shape. "Awed" reading of Kierkegaard and Heidegger' (Bennington, p. 328). Elsewhere (*Points de suspension*, p. 306), you wrote that Sartre represented for you a necessary but insufficient problematic, too historico-sociological and metaphysical at the same time.

Derrida.   At a certain point I thought I had to distance myself from what was called 'philosophy of existence'. It was when I began to read a little more seriously, but my intention was certainly not to draw away from the concern for existence itself, for concrete personal commitment, or for the existential pathos that, in a sense, I have never lost. Rather, what I did stemmed from my critical reflections on the reading of Husserl and Heidegger advanced by certain French existentialists such as Sartre and Marcel; and my dissent did not mean, of course, that I turned my back on existential questions. In some way, a philosopher without this ethico-existential pathos does not interest me very much, and basically the sense of desire and commitment I had when I read Rousseau, Nietzsche or Gide as a very young man is still with me.

But it is Kierkegaard to whom I have been most faithful and who interests me most: absolute existence, the meaning he gives to the word subjectivity, the resistance of existence to the concept or the system – this is something I attach great importance to and feel very deeply, something I am always ready to stand up for. Ultimately, even that which some people thought they could interpret as a reduction of philosophy to literature, as a way of reducing the philosophical to the literary, stems from that gesture. It is not that I find literature desirable for its own sake, but that for me it also represents this singularity of experience and of existence in its link to language. In literature what always interests me is essentially the autobiographical – not what is called the 'autobiographical genre', but rather the autobiographicity that greatly overflows the 'genre' of autobiography. Indeed, I find the vast majority of autobiographical novels not nearly autobiographical enough. Thus I try to focus on that which in the autobiographical exceeds the literary genre, the discursive genre, and even the *autos* [the self/same]; I try to interrogate that which in the *autos* disturbs self-relation, but always in an existential experience that is singular, and if not ineffable at least untranslatable or on the verge of untranslatability. It is as if I were always trying to provoke someone to translate something that escapes or refuses translation.

Memoirs, in a form that does not correspond to what are generally called memoirs, are the general form of everything that interests me – the wild desire to preserve everything, to gather everything together in its idiom. To gather together even that which disseminates and, by its very essence, defies all gathering. And philosophy, or academic philosophy at any rate, for me has always been at the service of this autobiographical design of memory. This, however, does not mean renouncing the specificity of the philosophical genre, the specifically philosophical demand – what it attests to is the desire, while taking philosophical responsibility to its limits, to show that such responsibility cannot be other than the responsibility *of someone*. Formalizing this to the extreme, I would say that for me the great question is always the question *who*. Call it biographical, autobiographical or existential, the form of the question *who* is what matters to me, be it in, say, its Kierkegaardian, Nietzschean, or Heideggerian form. *Who? Who asks the question who? Where? How? When? Who arrives?* It is always the most difficult question, the irreducibility of *who* to *what*, or the place where between *who* and *what* the limit trembles, in some way. It is clear that the *who* withdraws from or provokes the displacement of the

categories in which biography, autobiography, and memoirs
are thought. Abyssal question of the signature, but also signature of the question, the pledge pledged in the question.

Ferraris.   1949–50. 'First trip to "metropolitan" France, first
trip at all.' (Bennington, p. 328)

Derrida.   Until I was 19 I had never been away from
Algiers, not more than 80 or 100 kilometres at any rate.
Absolutely sedentary. Since then, even if there have been
quite a number of them, my trips have always had to do
with academic matters. I am not a traveller, I have a taste
for the sedentary. On occasion I have dreamed of travelling
without academic appointments of any kind, but I don't do
it, or very rarely.

Ferraris.   But there is a photo of a trip to Normandy, in
1956, with Robert Abirached.

Derrida.   Yes, but even that was a sort of academic trip. I
went to Normandy with that old car from 1930, my first
car, and the first car owned by a student at the Ecole
Normale; I'd bought it together with a friend of mine, for
600 francs. It was just before the teacher's examination
[*concours d'agrégation*], I was very tired, and worried sick as
I always was on the eve of that sort of exam; so I had gone
to rest in a house that a banker put at the disposal of intellectuals who were *découragé*.
   Even when I began to take very long trips I always stayed
in school. Even when I'm abroad I'm still in the university,
and that must mean something. Despite my uneasiness, my
malaise, despite my sense of not belonging to the Ecole
Normale, and before that to the *lycée*, to the *khâgn* [pre-
paratory course] for the Ecole Normale, and later to any
university institution whatsoever – despite all that I was
marked, and I accepted the marks left by what they taught
me to do in *khâgn* and at the Ecole Normale. Even if I
protested against that discipline, against the unspoken norms
of the discipline of reading, it's true that they continue to

inspire in me an ineradicable respect. Those models of philological, micrological, I'd say even grammatico-logical demands, for me have never lost their irrecusable authority. The rest came along to complicate matters, but it is as if a certain grammar had been given for ever. Things do get sorted out later on, but you still preserve that legacy, however much you question and contest it. It is like a language you can denounce only in your own language, which is *that same* language. Even when I give the impression of transgressing, putting into question, displacing, it is always under their authority, with a sense of responsibility in the face of a certain philological morality, before a certain ethics of reading or of writing. In short: before the law.

Ferraris. 'I will speak, therefore, of the letter *a*, this first letter which it apparently has been necessary to insinuate, here and there, into the writing of the word *difference*; and to do so in the course of a writing on writing, and also of a writing within writing whose different trajectories thereby find themselves, at certain very determined points, intersecting with a kind of gross spelling mistake' (*Margins of Philosophy*, p. 3).

Derrida.   I detest grammatical mistakes. Even when I take liberties that some people find provocative, I do so with the feeling – justifiable or not – that I do in fact know the rules. A transgression should always know what it transgresses, which always makes the transgression impure, and compromised in advance with what it transgresses.

I am someone who has never left university. I know, there are times I feel I have not left it enough, and other times – sometimes at the same time – I think I did well to stay. So I have this attitude that some people must have perceived as double, of emancipation, revolt, irony, and at the same time of scrupulous fidelity. And I feel best when my sense of emancipation preserves the memory of what it emancipates from. I hope this mingling of respect and disrespect for the academic heritage and tradition in general is legible in everything I do. I think this is the crux of the double law

I spoke of, the profoundly sedentary nature of someone who travels a great deal.

Ferraris.   1952–3. Entering the Ecole Normale Supérieure.

Derrida.   It was in the early 1950s that phenomenology first gained a sort of academic legitimacy, thanks especially to Merleau-Ponty. But Husserl was not really being read in the universities. Phenomenology had made its way into France, though principally through channels extrinsic to science; which is to say, through the phenomenology of perception, anthropology and Sartrean ontology. However, at bottom, questions of epistemology, reflections on the history of science, on mathematical idealities – none of this had been taken into account. What I recall about my first years at the Ecole Normale is being caught up in that effervescence which was Marxist and epistemological at the same time; there were Foucault's courses on Merleau-Ponty, on *Ideen II*. Reading Husserl, I said to myself that it was necessary to go back to those aspects of his work that had largely been overlooked in France, namely the question of science, of the stratum of scientific judgements, of history, and all in connection with what Tran Duc Thao was doing, in his attempt to hinge phenomenology on dialectical materialism. This accounts for the choice I made in my early work on Husserl, which was to privilege the Husserl of genetic constitution, the genesis of mathematical objects, the genesis of objectivity and science. And it was here, in a context whose history ought to be reconstructed, that the gap first opened between my ideas and the Sartrean and Merleau-Pontian tradition of phenomenology.

In that period Althusser was at the Ecole Normale – he wasn't teaching very much at the time, but was a well-known Marxist – and Foucault, who was teaching courses on Merleau-Ponty and on aphasia, on Goldstein, pathology, the phantom limb etc., and of course all this played a role in the form my interest in phenomenology took. It must be said that in that period we greatly admired a man about whom hardly anyone now talks: I'm thinking of Martial Guéroult, a historian of philosophy who was very meticulous, very demanding in his reconstruction of the internal logic of systems, for example of the order of reasons in Descartes – a structural reading all his own, independent of the biographical, of the Cartesian novel, that attempted to reconstruct the chain of reasoning step by step. He was a model for many of us; we tried to read a text the way Guéroult did. I'm not sure I'm as convinced today as I was then, but at that time our model was this type of reading that reconstructed the internal concatenation of a system, step by step and with the maximum care for detail. So there was this very French model of philosophy *à la* Guéroult, and then this Husserl that we began to wrest away from the authority of Sartre and Merleau-Ponty.

In Guéroult's model, then, there was a respect for the way the text works, for the logic of the philosophemes without taking the author into account, and a concern with reconstructing the greatest coherence possible in a systematic arrangement of philosophemes, as well as an attention to the way the text works formally; it was not a question of subscribing or not subscribing to a thesis or of philosophizing for its own sake, but of seeing how things *worked* – a sort of philosophical technology. At the same time, there was an attention to the letter, to literality: not to the breath that breathes through a text, to what it *means*, but to its literal working, its functioning. Whatever the doubts I may have about it now, this model wielded great authority over me, even if at a certain point I contested it; still, it was the contestation of someone who recognized the great value of what he was contesting. This accounts for my sympathy for structuralism, even if, as you know, I raised questions and voiced disagreements. But basically I have a great deal of respect for that which appears to me always necessary and legitimate in the reading of a text, culture, system or configuration.

It is in this context that I took my first trip outside France – the first time that I crossed a border, because between Algeria and France the Mediterranean was not yet a national border. In 1954 I went to Louvain to consult some unpublished works of Husserl's, his works on time, because I was working on the genetic constitution of the ego. So it was the very first of my philosophical journeys.

Ferraris.   In 1967 *Speech and Phenomena, Writing and Difference* and *Of Grammatology* were published, and in 1972 *Dissemination, Margins of Philosophy* and *Positions*. There is a notable difference between the first and the second trilogy, at least formally.

Derrida.   Although the texts published in 1972 seem relatively heterogeneous with respect to those of 1967, the work was marked by great continuity. Speaking figuratively, the seism is a good image for what I mean: the moment of a seism has been prepared for a very long time by invisible micro-displacements in the earth. And then at a certain point, from our point of view, there is what we call an earthquake; but the earthquake, from the point of view *of the earth*, is nothing. 'Plato's Pharmacy' was written in 1968–9, the year after *On Grammatology*, and was nothing more than an elaboration upon a remark in *Grammatology* on the *pharmakon*. If anyone found it amusing to follow this game or this necessity, they would discover that there is not a single text of mine that was not precisely, literally and explicitly announced ten or twenty years beforehand. When I began publishing, in the early 1960s, I had already written that text on Husserl ten years before; in everything I've published there are always touchstones announcing what I would like to write about later on – even ten or twenty years later on, as I said. I have a feeling not just of continuity but of a sort of immobility, a movement *sur place*. The question of writing was already announced in my higher-studies dissertation of 1954.

This motion *sur place* does not prevent me from being constantly surprised, from having a feeling of being always on the verge . . .

Ferraris.   'It was in 1966, during a symposium in the United States we were both participating in. After some friendly remarks about the talk I had just given, Jean Hyppolite added: "That said, I really don't see where you are going." I think I answered him more or less like this: "If I saw clearly, and beforehand, where I was going, I really think I would not take even one more step to get there" ' (*Du droit à la philosophie*, p. 442).

Derrida. Every time I write something, I have the impression of making a beginning – but in fact that which is the same in texture is ceaselessly exposed to a singularity which is that of the other (another text, someone else, another word of the language). Everything appears *anew:* which means newness and repetition together. What, for me, ceaselessly repeats itself is my surprise in the face of what I have not yet done and which is still virgin and intact; whatever I begin to write, even in the case of small, relatively unimportant things, I always have the same slightly anxious feeling that I mustn't count on anything I've said before, that I have to start all over again. In the actual writing, of course I'm well aware of the fact that at bottom it all unfolds according to the same law that commands these always different things. It may be ascribed to ingenuousness or presumption, foolhardiness or forgetfulness, but it's true that when I write I never get bored. Never being bored while repeating the same thing all the time – this is a real problem. I can only hope that what I say about philosophy, literature, the event, the signature, and iterability (altering-altered repetition) is consistent with our encountering this ever renewed singularity. I try to think that *tout autre est tout autre* [every other is wholly other]. To remain within the experience of teaching, which for me is very important because it permits me to speak and write at a rhythm more in keeping with my breathing, the texts that I read and reread are always completely new to me. At the moment I'm teaching Heidegger and I really do have the feeling of reading *Being and Time* for the first time in my life; and what is true of Heidegger is true of Plato, Kant – everyone. It is also a certain amnesia that accounts for this taste of mine, which may be considered a strength or a weakness. I won't say that I know how to forget, but I do know that I forget, and that this is not entirely a bad thing even if I suffer for it. I must have a rather peculiar way of teaching, which explains the mistrust or rejection on the part of some students, but at the same time – why deny it? – the interest and fidelity of a great many others. This depends in part on the fact that I have never renounced that discipline we spoke of earlier; my teaching is always based on it, and on trying to transmit a respect for it: close reading of the texts, reference to the original, to the letter, patience, slowness. In short, a respect for the classical virtues of teaching (which, alas, are not widespread) and of the reading of canonical – or canonized – texts, even though this does not stop me from reading other texts, or from continually problematizing the authority behind the process of canonization.

It is true, however, that this respect cohabits with something that would appear to contradict it, with a sort of madness or freedom. It's true that the *mise-en-scène* of this superegoistic, patient and microscopic reading can appear a bit baroque or provocative at times. But I play by these rules. The testimonial I always like best is when a student comes to me and says: 'Well, now I feel like working on my own and writing when I hadn't felt like it any more; the classics had started to bore me, but now I really feel like reading them.'

Ferraris. 1968. 'J. D. appears somewhat withdrawn or even reserved about some aspects of the May 1968 movement'; 1974. 'Drafts the *"Avant-projet* for the foundation of the Groupe de recherche sur l'enseignement philosophique" (Greph) and founds this group with friends, colleagues and students, the following year'; 1979. 'Along with others, takes the initiative of organizing the Estates General of Philosophy held at the Sorbonne'; 1980. 'Defence of a *Thèse d'Etat* at the Sorbonne'; 1981. 'With Jean-Pierre Vernant and some friends, founds the Jan Hus Association [...] The same year, goes to Prague to run a clandestine seminar [...] he is imprisoned on the charge of "production and trafficking of drugs"'; 1983. 'Foundation of the Collège international de philosophie [. . .] Elected to the Ecole des hautes études en sciences sociales (director of studies: *Philosophical Institutions*)' (Bennington, pp. 332–5).

Derrida. An overview of this sequence gives the impression, which I think is justified, that in my work I pose the question of the institution more and more, in terms of both theory and practice, and in accordance with premises that, moreover, have been present for a very long time. (Everything that links deconstruction to the question of the apparatus of the institution is already present in *Of Grammatology.*) This logic has come to have a progressively greater impact on my life, my actions, and my institutional inscription, which has taken the form of a widening gap as far as the givens of my institutionality are concerned. (I deliberately reject the idea of writing a thesis after 1968; with others, I found the 'Greph' in 1975, after having drafted the preliminary programme and proposed the group's creation; I multiply my acts of opposition to the given philosophical institution.) But at the same time the philosophical institution becomes a theme of my work, the logic of which led me in the end to propose as the organizing theme at the Ecole des hautes études en sciences sociales, in 1983, 'Philosophical Institutions'. So here we have a movement that possesses, at the same time, an internal logic and a form of response to critical situations and socio-political conditions in France: for example the 'Greph', which had its internal logic and necessity, also gave an immediate response, in the here and now, to a very particular 'contingency', the 'Haby' reform programme, which effectively threatened to wipe out the teaching of philosophy in the *lycées*, the scandal of a report by a board of examiners that in fact was the origin of the foundation of the 'Greph' – after a letter I had written myself, etc.

In 1968 I had the impression that the action of the students (which was not that of the workers) to provoke the revolution was unrealistic, and that it could have dangerous consequences, as in fact it did two months later with the election of the most right-wing Chamber of Deputies we had ever had in France – before the current one, that is. The strategy was not the best one possible; it was necessary to free our-selves from the programmes of the political parties and the unions simultaneously – but I did not say no to "68', I took part in the demonstrations, I organized the first general assembly at the Ecole Normale. Still, rightly or wrongly, my heart was not 'on the barricades'. What really bothered me was not so much the apparent spontaneity, which I do not believe in, but the spontaneist political eloquence, the call for transparency, for communication without relay or delay, the liberation from any sort of apparatus, party or union.

The mistrust with regard to all those things that I witnessed in 1968 corresponded not only to a philosophico-political position, but also to what was already, for me, a sort of crypto-communist legacy, namely the condemnation of 'spontaneism' in Lenin's *What Is To Be Done?* In rereading Lenin's texts recently, in an altogether different context, I rediscovered this critique of spontaneism. In abstract and general terms, what remains constant in my thinking on this question is indeed a critique of institutions, but one that sets out not from the utopia of a wild and spontaneous pre- or non-institution, but rather from counter-institutions. I do not think there is, or should be, the 'non-institutional'. I am always torn be-tween the critique of institutions and the dream of an *other* institution that, in an interminable process, will come to replace institutions that are oppressive, violent and inoperat-ive. The idea of a counter-institution, neither spontaneous, wild nor immediate, is the most permanent motif that, in a way, has guided me in my work. What I try to explain, for example in *Du droit à la philosophie*, is that the philosoph-ical as such, which is not meta-institutional, is nevertheless a very paradoxical institution, whose space has to be admin-istrated without a symmetrical contract – an institution in which thought on the subject of the institutionality of the institution has to remain open and have a future [*avenir*]. Of course, it will be said that deconstruction of the question of the institution is not institutionalizable – but neither does it belong to a space untouched by institutionality. It is prob-ably this logic that has guided me for all these years, always at war with institutions, but always attempting to found yet another one – the 'Greph', then the Etats généraux and the Collège, all of them counter-institutions with original and paradoxical ideas (albeit unrealized) on the subject of counter-institutionality. I have even had occasion to define the State – the State as it ought to be – as a counter-institution, necessary for opposing those institutions that represent particular interests and properties. And I'd say the same thing with regard to international law.

I also think that what happened in Prague, the Jan Hus society, the fact that I went to see them and ended up in prison, follows from the same logic: creating an association that helps dissidents pursue their work in philosophy, even though the people of Charta '77 were not essentially anti-constitutionalists. Charta said: we are in favour of respecting the constitution, and at present the repression, in its legal form, does not respect it. This means that the Jan Hus association set itself limits: we will not make a revolution in Prague, we will not overthrow the established authority; not immediately; but we will help those who want to continue philosophical work, intellectuals and writers whose Charta is precisely respect for the constitution; we will help make the institution revolt against itself, against the abuse of power that perverts it.

Ferraris.   In *The Post Card* you tell of a dream about the Resistance.

Derrida.   Naturally my heroic phantasms – I think this is true for many Frenchmen and Frenchwomen of my generation – usually have to do with the period of the Resistance, which I did not experience firsthand; I wasn't old enough, and I wasn't in France. When I was very young – and until quite recently – I used to project a film in my mind of someone who, by night, plants bombs on the railway: blowing up the enemy structure, planting the delayed-action device and then watching the explosion or at least hearing it from a distance. I see very well that this image, which translates a deep phantasmic compulsion, could be illustrated by deconstructive operations, which consist in planting discreetly, with a

delayed-action mechanism, devices that all of a sudden put
a transit route out of commission, making the enemy's movements more hazardous. But the friend, too, will have to live
and think differently, know where he's going, tread lightly.

Ferraris. 'This is, beyond the philosophical scope of propositions, a purely literary effect, the new *frisson*, the poetry
of Derrida. When I read him, I always recall the exodus of
1940. A retreating military unit arrives in an as yet unsus-
pecting locality, where cafés are open, where the ladies
visit the "ladies' fashion store", where the hairdressers dress
hair and bakers bake; where viscounts meet other viscounts
and tell each other stories of viscounts, and where, an hour
later, everything is deconstructed and devastated' (Emmanuel
Lévinas, *Proper Names*, 'Wholly Otherwise', trans. Simon
Critchley, p. 4).

Derrida. A few weeks ago a friend of mine, Samuel Weber,
brought this text to my attention, saying: 'Doesn't it bother
you? Look at what they're accusing you of now. You're like
the enemy army!' At that point I reread Lévinas's text,
which is in fact generous in my regard; but when you see
what he says, I mean, that when I passed through it was as
if the German army had hit town, there was nothing left . . . it
makes you wonder. It's bizarre, I'd never looked at the text
from that angle. What is the unconscious of that image?
And then the Nazi invader . . . It's sort of like the Resistance
dream we spoke about, but turned upside down.

Ferraris. Your resistance to photography lasted until 1979.
Foucault wrote, in *The Archaeology of Knowledge*, that quite
a number of people, himself definitely included, write in
order to no longer have a face.

Derrida. There were several different reasons for my refusal
to be photographed, which did last a long time. One of them,
a profound one, unquestionably has to do with being ill at
ease with my own image — the relation to death that one reads

in every portrait, the dissimulation of the face in writing, the problem I always have, for that matter, with my own face.⟩The other explanation, regarding my refusal of public photography, has a political basis: it was a question of resistance to the rules that organize promotion in the 'culture market'. Authors had their pictures taken in stereotyped poses, the professor or the writer with the books behind them, etc. I had absolutely nothing against the art of photography, I just wanted to protest against the culture market and what it did with the image of authors. I remember when they were preparing that special issue of *Arc* about me [no. 54, 1973] – I said I didn't want any photos, which very nearly sank the whole project, since an issue like that was supposed to have a photo of the author in question on the cover. They did cave in in the end – they put that reptile of Escher's on the cover and it sold very well, but there really had been a problem. It was a war. I felt that the author should not appear, it was ridiculous, vulgar, and inconsistent with the very things I had written about authors. Even now that I've practically given up resisting – because it's effectively not possible, and besides it's too late – I don't have a clear conscience about it.

Since the early 1980s the question of photography has become relatively secondary – now we have the big question of television, which has taken its place. So far, I have managed to be faithful to my rule that I will agree to appear on television only when the cause in question has nothing whatsoever to do with promoting my books. On my way back from Czechoslovakia I was interviewed in the train, and then there was the time we created the Collège international de philosophie.

Ferraris. 1984. 'Frankfurt: lecture at Habermas's seminar and opening address at the Joyce conference in Frankfurt' (Bennington, p. 307). 'Derrida is particularly interested in standing the primacy of logic over rhetoric, canonized since Aristotle, on its head' (Jürgen Habermas, *The Philosophical Discourse of Modernity*, trans. Frederick Lawrence, p. 187).

Derrida. I have had occasion to say that deconstruction is a project in favour of the Enlightenment [*les Lumières*], and that one must not confuse the Enlightenment of the eighteenth century with the Enlightenment of tomorrow. But I think it was wrong to get involved in such a confused debate, where one speaks of *Lumières* in general, as if Enlightenment, *Aufklärung, Illuminismo, Lumières* were all the same thing. The right thing, which unfortunately I did not do, would have been not to accept a debate for or against 'Enlightenment' *tout court*, but rather to differentiate each time, to state *which* Enlightenment I'm talking about, what the 'light' of the Enlightenment is, and *what* Enlightenment I'm in favour of. The same holds for the concept of revolution or of conservation. A sort of 'sloganization' has taken hold of the debate. In general the debates between Germany and France, Habermas or the succession of the Frankfurt School and then 'the French', are a journalistic degradation of debates that ought to be more serious, sharper, more refined in their consciousness and historical memory.

I think that when philosophers speak of argument they very often have a certain model of argument in mind, and when they fail to recognize that familiar model, they hasten to conclude that there *is no* argument. I myself say, rather, that there *is* argument, in another form. I think that literature is argumentative, in another way, with different procedures. Literature attempts to lead to conclusions, even if they are suspensive or undecidable; it is an organized discourse that exchanges with the other, needs the response of the other, is discursive, and therefore passes through a temporality. Such argumentation does not obey the norms of philosophy, even supposing – and it is still a presupposition – that within philosophy there is only one type of argumentation. All the discussions between philosophers throughout history are not only discussions – thus, argumentations – about theses or thetic contents, but are also about argumentative norms. Kant critiques the way in which Descartes argues and the fact that he is not faithful to what argumentation *ought* to be, according to Kant. Intraphilosophical discussion is a discussion about argumentation. Aristotle says to Plato: here you are no longer *arguing*. If within philosophy itself there is no consensus on the subject of argumentation, one has to accept the fact that outside of philosophy the same dissent exists. There is a great ensemble, which we call philosophy, where multiple argumentations appear to occupy a space assigned them by a general contract; but not even this is certain, and it could be shown that there is literature within philosophy. *Aufhebung* is a poetic signature in its own right. Someone who doesn't speak German, who doesn't accept this, would say: 'He tells me there is an operation that means, at the same time, destroy and preserve, lift up and suppress – this is not arguing, we no longer know what we are talking about, the misunderstanding has to be reduced before we can discuss anything, etc.'

I take seriously the axiom that there is a philosophical *locus*, that there is a type of philosophical discourse or demand, and I attempt to go as far as possible with respect to this specificity (which is always to come, which is not given in any place). But at the same time I think that this thought of a philosophical limit, the border of this locus, also has its limit, is also a problem: philosophy fails to be what it wants to be. So this locus is a place of disputation – a disputed place in the sense that there is dispute about it, it is in discussion, but also in the sense that it is a place one wants to occupy, that one wants to appropriate, a place that one disputes etc. It is a place that carries within itself the law of its displacement, of its internal heterogeneity. Taking up the figure of the seism once again, there is an underground fault that works the philosophical soil. Taking an interest in the philosophical locus, I also take an interest in this fault, which is responsible for the fact that, at more or less regular intervals, there are earthquakes, there are events. For there to be an event there has to be a place, which then has to be overflowed, put into question, fissured; respect for the axiom in question enjoins me to pay attention to what in this place is *unheimlich*. Philosophy has a way of being at home with itself [*chez elle*] that consists in not being at home with itself, whence this double bind with respect to the philosophical. This explains many of the reactions to my work. People think

I don't take philosophy seriously or that I confuse philosophy with something else, but then at the same time that I am too meticulous, too literalist a philosopher, and they can't come to terms with this mixture of religious respect and miscreance.

Ferraris.   1989. 'Opening address to the large colloquium organized by the Cardozo School of Law in New York [. . .] on *Deconstruction and the Possibility of Justice*' (Bennington, p. 335).

Derrida.   It could be shown that there was nothing I said on that occasion that wasn't included in my earlier texts. Nonetheless, in an American space, the ambit of 'critical legal studies' (a political theory of right [*droit*] related to deconstruction), and thus on juridical territory, among jurists, I said for the first time in so many words that *there is an indeconstructible*, and that justice is indeconstructible. A great number of things followed from the logic of that statement. The distinction between right [*droit*] and justice, for instance. Reading Benjamin's text on the subject helped me articulate my position, which was to become the matrix of a great many discourses I formulated later on – *Specters of Marx* moves in that direction, inspired by an idea of justice irreducible to that of right. I recalled that powerful statement by Lévinas, 'the relation to the other, i.e. justice', which says something analogous in so few words. The relation to the singularity of the other is not assimilated by right. The logic of the gift is not reducible to the logic of restitution. Right, whose history is eminently deconstructible, is restitution, redistribution, equivalence, whereas justice exceeds all that and supposes dislocation. Justice – going back to Hamlet's phrase, which also plays an important role in *Specters of Marx* – is 'out of joint', *aus den Fugen*. This is the crux of my debate with Heidegger, when in his powerful text on the Anaximander fragment he places *dikē* on the side of the *Fuge*, the joint, adjustment, conjunction. My response is that what is needed is disjunction – that disjunction, which can be evil, is nonetheless the condition of justice. Deconstruction is justice, in the disproportion between the other and myself, between myself and myself as other.

Ferraris. 'Be it with or without psychoanalytical *arrière-pensées*, one can still pose questions about this axiomatic condition of interpretative discourse that Professor Gadamer calls *Verstehen,* "understanding the other", "understanding one another". Whether one speaks of consensus or of misunderstanding (Schleiermacher), one may still wonder whether the condition for *Verstehen,* far from being the continuum of the "relation" [. . .] is not rather the interruption of the relation, a certain relation of interruption, the suspension of all mediation' ('Bonnes volontés de puissance. Une réponse à Hans-Georg Gadamer', p. 343).

Derrida.   In consensus, in possible transparency, the secret is never broached/breached [*entamé*]. If I am to share something, to communicate, objectify, thematize, the condition is that there be something non-thematizable, non-objectifiable, non-sharable. And this 'something' is an absolute secret, it is the *ab-solutum* itself in the etymological sense of the term, i.e., that which is cut off from any bond, detached, and which cannot itself bind; it is the condition of any bond but it cannot bind itself to anything – this is the absolute, and if there is something absolute it is secret. It is in this direction that I try to read Kierkegaard, the sacrifice of Isaac, the absolute as secret and as *tout autre* [wholly other]. Not transcendent, not even beyond myself, but a 'making appear' to me: a resistance to the daylight of phenomenality that is radical, irreversible, to which any sort of form may be given – death, for example, though it is not death either.

From this point of view the autobiographical is the locus of the secret, but not in the sense – as some would have it – that it holds the key to a secret, be it conscious or unconscious. Yes, there is a secret of that sort, but it is not the secret that I attempt to think, i.e., to put into a formalizable, expressible relation with everything that it is not. What is the place of this *unconditional* and *absolute* secret in a space where either there is no secret, or secrets are negotiable – secrets that can be hidden, things that are preserved, that are placed in reserve.

Clearly, the most tempting figure for this absolute/secret is death, that which has a relation to death, that which is carried off by death – that which is thus life itself. Now, it is true that the relation to death is a privileged dimension of this experience of the secret, *but I imagine that an immortal would have the same experience*. Even for an immortal this secret would be concealed, sealed. Fundamentally, everything I attempt to do, think, teach and write has its raison d'être, spur, calling and appeal in this secret, which interminably disqualifies any effort one can make to determine it. As I have attempted to show in <u>Given</u> *Time* and in *Passions*, we never finish with this secret, we are never finished, there is no end.

Somehow, this secret that we *speak* of but are unable to *say* is, paradoxically, like good sense in Descartes, the best-shared thing in the world; but it is the sharing of what is not shared: we know in common that we have nothing in common. There may be an unlimited consensus on the subject, but the consensus is of no use, since it is a consensus on the fact that the singular is singular, that the other is other, that *tout autre est tout autre*. As far as this formula is concerned, I think that everyone agrees, no one can seriously protest against it or rebut it, but it makes no difference – *difference*, the differend, and consequently a war and polemics are not only possible, they are *the necessary result* of this agreement that *tout autre est tout autre*. And so this consensus means neither agreement, nor peace, nor order – there is a consensus on *nothing*, on the fact that everything that exists shares the unsharable. This type of formula is then, perhaps, the model of those *x*'s that define the *Geschäft der Philosophie* – here, the only history possible is one of philosophical dissensions and dissents: the history of philosophy as a history of dis-agreement and divisions about this same that is not the same.

Why elect the word 'secret' to say this? Why privilege this word rather than the word *same*, or *logos*, or *being*? The choice is not insignificant: it is a strategy, in a definite philosophical scene, that wishes to insist on separation, isolation.

Between *this* secret and what is generally called secret, even if the two are heterogeneous, there is an analogy that makes me prefer the secret to the non-secret, the secret to the public expression, exhibition, phenomenality. I have a taste for the secret, it clearly has to do with not-belonging; I have an impulse of fear or terror in the face of a political space, for example, a public space that makes no room for the secret. For me, the demand that everything be paraded in the public square and that there be no internal forum is a glaring sign of the totalitarianization of democracy. I can rephrase this in terms of political ethics: if a right to the secret is not maintained, we are in a totalitarian space.

Belonging – the fact of avowing one's belonging, of putting in common – be it family, nation, tongue – spells the loss of the secret.

Paris, 25–6 January 1994

IV

Hope arrives finally at the conclusion *that something is* (which determines the ultimate possible end) *because something ought to happen*; knowing, *that something is* (which operates as the supreme cause) *because something happens.*
                    Kant, *Critique of Pure Reason*, B834/A806, trans.
                                        Norman Kemp Smith

Derrida. [Opening oneself to what comes can be a way of exposing oneself to the future [*à l'avenir*] or to the coming of the other, to the coming of what does not depend on me.] Consequently, this exposure is under the law of the singularity of the other. It may also be thought under the category of the *kairos*, or of chance (the aleatory), which are not exactly the same thing, although they do intersect.

Ferraris. What, then, is the relation between the incalculable and calculation, chance and strategy? Yesterday I asked you why you chose to write a book on Marx, and you answered: because there was a conference. And if it had been a conference on Hitler?

Derrida. The conference on Marx might not have taken place, and in that case perhaps I would not have written that book on Marx; I hesitated, and I tried to ask myself whether responding on that occasion was strategically well calculated. There was a long period of deliberation, but at the end of the day, whatever the calculation might have been, there came a time when I said 'let's accept', and I accepted. Chance, then, does come into play; but, clearly, it could be demonstrated that this chance could only have presented itself at the end of an extremely complicated chain, linked to me, linked to the academic and political scenes, and to a thousand causalities we could attempt to analyse, to show that this chance, though still by chance, is inscribed in an extremely rigorous concatenation.

Perhaps my most fully articulated thinking on the subject is in ['Mes chances', where I tried to say what I mean by this value of the aleatory. But the densest knot where this question is concerned is a knot that not only knots together each time, in a single conjuncture, the aleatory, alterity and calculative rationality. A decision has to be prepared by reflection and knowledge, but the moment of the decision, and thus the moment of responsibility, supposes a rupture with knowledge, and therefore an opening to the incalculable – a sort of 'passive' decision. In other words, one cannot rationally distribute the part [*part*] that is calculable and the part that is incalculable. One has to calculate as far as possible, but the incalculable happens [*arrive*]: it is the other, and singularity, and chance, without one's being able to do one's part [*part*]; the parting [*partage*: distribution] between reason and its other, the calculable and the incalculable, the necessary and the aleatory, is without example; it does not obey a logic of distinction, it is not a parting with two parts.

If it is not a parting – a division into shares, or a distribution into parts – then the space of rationality can be totally invaded by or surrendered to what we call the incalculable, chance, the other, the event. *Here* is the enigma of this situation in which I get lost; but it is *this* enigma that erases the difference between calculative rationality and its other; and *this* enigma complicates and entangles all questions of decision and responsibility. One has to know, one has to know it. But, since the moment in which the decision is made is heterogeneous to knowing, I say it very firmly and unconditionally, but I inscribe this unconditionality on the trembling non-limit that I have just said. And I could, naturally, give a great many examples; it is the law of everything I write and of everything that happens to me [*qui m'arrive*]. Each time I write a text, it is 'on occasion', occasional, for some occasion. I have never planned to write a text; everything I've done, even the most composite of my books, were 'occasioned' by a question. My concern with the date and the signature confirms it.

Right now, since you and I are talking together in a hotel room in Naples there is a point in the text that I am writing – it's there on the table behind you – where, though I am speaking of psychoanalysis, archives, Freud, religion etc., in a discussion of Freud's *Gradiva* I remark that I am writing this in sight of Pompeii, at this moment, etc. I have the impression that if I were to efface these traces, these archives of the occasion, I would lose my life, I would make it even more ephemeral and neutralized. I want, if possible, to mark even the most speculative of thoughts with a language and with a date: this came to me, at exactly that moment.

Ferraris.   Here, however, deconstruction portrays a thought even weaker than the 'pensiero debole'/'weak thought' of Vattimo or Rorty, and hypertolerant as well: accept my contingency, I'll do the same for yours. Not that this would be the worst of situations: as Rorty puts it, when all is said and done, better professors than torturers. But it is also true that the inquisitor who burns books – and sometimes their authors – is more respectful of their theses than is the case in the contingent, *solidaire* and ironic republic of ideas.

Derrida.   The fact that I never use the word 'tolerance' is not fortuitous. Some friends asked me to participate in Geneva in a conference on the idea of tolerance, on Voltaire, and they wanted to transform the conference – which was academic at first – into a militant act of protest against all manifestations of intolerance in the world, from the Rushdie affair to the intellectuals who have been assassinated practically all over the world. I wasn't able to go, but I sent a little text in which I suggested, referring to the article entitled 'Tolérance' in Voltaire's *Dictionnaire philosophique*, that it's best to be prudent with this concept of tolerance. Voltaire's

text is magnificent, but it also makes me quite uneasy. It is
an Enlightenment text, which refers above all to the duty of
Christians, confident in their faith, to tolerate others. Thus
it implies at once relativism and dogmatism: 'We are sure of
our faith, so we'll leave the others alone, even if they're in
error; we won't persecute them.' And this idea of tolerating
others, of putting up with their difference, while knowing
full well that it's we who are in the right, I find at once
dogmatic and relativistic, both non-relativistic and relativistic.
And, as you suggested yourself, I would see in certain cases
of this sort a form of disrespect. If the concept of tolerance
is given a very sharp sense, then to be sure I hope to be
tolerant, but I would prefer to find another word and another
concept to give such precision to what I think has to be the
opening to the other, respect for the other. If we had time,
I would try to propose a deconstructive genealogy of the concept of tolerance, and then see how one could go beyond it.
Now, there is no deconstruction that does not start with the
attempt to respect a text or discourse. That said, it is certainly
not a question of destroying the text or belief or thought of
the other, nor of belittling it in any way. In this regard, I'd
like to go back to what you said earlier about deconstruction
as thought even weaker than so-called 'weak thought'. I think
it's true, in a certain sense. If 'weak' implies liberal relativism,
then no, certainly not; but if it implies a certain disarming
quality in one's relation to the other, then yes, in that sense
yes: in a great number of my texts you will find a discourse
on weakness. A weakness that can transform itself into the
greatest strength. But there is a moment of absolute weakness and disarmament, and what we said earlier about the
occasion, chance, the aleatory, ultimately means exposing
ourselves to what we cannot appropriate: it is there, before
us, without us – *there* is someone, something, that happens,
that happens to us, and that has no need of us to happen (to
us). And this relation to the event or alterity, as well as to
chance or the occasion, leaves us completely disarmed; and
one has to be disarmed. The 'has to' says yes to the event: it
is stronger than I am; it was there before me; the 'has to' is
always the recognition of what is stronger than I.

(And there has to be a 'has to'. One has to have to. One
has to accept that 'it' [*ça*] (the other, or whatever 'it' may
be) is stronger than I am, for something to happen. I have
to lack a certain strength, I have to lack it enough, for
something to happen. If I were stronger than the other, or
stronger than what happens, nothing would happen.)There
has to be weakness, which is not perforce debility, imbecil-
ity, deficiency, malady or infirmity. Semantics is not sharp
enough to say this weakness; but there has to be a limit, and
the opening is a limit. This affirmation of weakness is unconditional; it is thus neither relativistic nor tolerant. And
as for those who will say just the opposite of what I've
just said, I think one has to oppose them firmly, not with
cowardly tolerance – even if, in a concrete situation, I usually think twice before opposing figures of liberalism and
tolerance.

Ferraris.   I continue to see the spectre of a philosophy of history or of a 'fatum mahometanum', which, furthermore, carries
in itself a contradiction:[to open oneself to the event is to open
oneself to everything,]except to the event of not-opening.

Derrida.   If by 'philosophy of history' one means a philosophy of providence, where history has an orientation – a
sense – then everything we have just said marks the limit
of such a philosophy. Where there is philosophy of history
there is no longer history, everything may in principle be
foreseen, everything is gathered in the gaze of a god or a
providence. Now, if there is a historicity, it supposes the limit
of a philosophy of history; a philosophy of history that takes
historicity into account is a contradiction. What I suggested
a moment ago was a thought of historicity: it exhausted the
very project of a philosophy of history – unless under the
name of 'philosophy of history' one opens things otherwise. If everything I am trying to say is a rupture with
philosophies of history, which from the Enlightenment to
Marx, via Hegel, have constituted our modern heritage, their
deconstruction is not itself the proposition of an ensemble
of theoretical propositions. I often say that deconstruction is
what happens [*ce qui arrive*]: the fact that 'it happens' [*ça*

arrive] is sufficient on its own to put philosophies of history into question.

Why write? I always have the feeling – at once very modest and hyperbolically presumptuous – that I have nothing to say. I don't feel I have anything in me that's interesting enough to authorize my saying 'here's the book I planned all by myself, without anyone asking me for it'. What presumption it takes to say 'here's what I think, what I write, and it deserves to be published and launched into the world'! And what tranquillity, to decide to publish something, to address a message to humanity! I always have a sort of sceptical and impatient smile for such things. What exonerates me, in part, from this suspicion of presumption is that I was *asked* to come, I was *asked* a question, and so I feel less ridiculous, less presumptuous, because I was 'answering' an occasion – I was responding politely to an invitation. Naturally this modesty, which is not feigned, is perfectly compatible with a sort of hyperbolic presumptuousness, which presumes that, at bottom, no matter what I say, it will be interesting. There will have been an occasion, it will be said that I spoke, and it will be remarked or remarkable: it 'makes' history, it makes events. It will not be interesting because I delivered a truth, but because I gave a *performance*. All these texts are performative performances, and it suffices that there be performative performance for the philosophy of history to find its limit: the philosophy of history says what there was, what there is, and what there will be, it makes no room for performance. And so as soon as there is something performative – as soon as something happens through discourse and in discourse – the philosophy of history is in trouble [*en panne*].

Ferraris. If it is true that in philosophy there are both animals (the philosophers) and zoologists (the historians of philosophy), in this taxonomy of the professional 'rational animal' you side without hesitation with the beasts.

Derrida. I think it's the same either way. Naturally there is a zoology that separates the philosophers into families, but it is an empirical ramification; I think that in fact every philosopher is both a historian and a speculative thinker. It is not possible to pose a philosophical question, however abstract and poor in history it may be, without having *already* begun to take its historicity into account. *Ti esti* is already charged with history.

Naturally, at this point there would be an enormous – and also historical – discourse to be developed on the way that the history of philosophy has become a discipline; there is a history of the history of philosophy, with some interesting mutations, but this does not mean that the history is non-speculative: neither the history of philosophy nor the history of the history of philosophy is devoid of speculation, and no speculation is devoid of history. In my own case, I'd say that I am incapable of distinguishing in what I do between the taking into account of the history of philosophy and a gesture that is not purely and simply historical. The concept of deconstruction is a historical concept, and at the same time it puts into question the concepts of historicity, of a history of truth.

Ferraris.   For pure theorizing (if it exists), the problem is the name: if one refers to an ideal Socrates, why call him Socrates?

Derrida.   There is a tradition in philosophy that, at regular intervals, repeats the gesture of the refusal of history. Every philosopher, each in his own way, started off by saying that it was time to be done with the history of philosophy. [Philosophy does not consist in telling stories: Plato said so, Heidegger said so. In the interim, every great philosopher began by saying: now we shall break with narrative and historical authority.]Take Descartes: reason is not memory; Kant did the same thing. Hegel is more of a historian than any of them, yet he proposes breaking with empirical history. Husserl too, evidently: even if he reintroduced a transcendental historicity later on, he began by doing away with historicity. Thus, in a sense, there is nothing more philosophical than the interruption of historical memory, and philosophers continually outdo one another in advocating ahistoricism.

All this helps explain why most philosophers came to the conclusion that proper names do not count: 'It's not because it was written by Plato that it's interesting'; and this is true, in a certain empirical context. But as soon as we take proper names and signatures seriously, things change; and taking proper names seriously means taking history seriously: the history of works [*oeuvres*], of the performative, of language (the fact that philosophy is bound up with natural languages). What is even more complicated is the paradoxical inscription of proper names in a language: the proper name is that which, in the language, is not part of the language, and is thus untranslatable. Taking the proper name seriously means taking seriously the oldest locus of resistance to the authority of translation; at the beginning of this conversation we spoke about opening to the other, about the fact that the other was there, and that there has to be a 'has to' by which I am disarmed before the other: this is what the proper name means. There was Socrates, there was Plato, absolutely singular moments that came before me, and that are the law; I have to try to respect the very thing that is untranslatable in the event that carries the name of Socrates. Weakness before the 'there has to be the other' passes in philosophy through the existence of proper names.

Ferraris. In 'Signature Event Context' [in *Margins of Philosophy*] you allude to the fact that *iter* and *alter* both come from the Sanskrit *itara*. How is it possible, not in language but in ontology, that iteration and alteration coincide? Kant spoke of a mystery deposited in the human soul, Husserl wrote that there is no name for it, but others will say that such answers are shots in the dark.

Derrida. Everything in my texts that is articulated under the name of iterability has something to do with the paradox you have just recalled. But the question is enormous and there's no way we can master it today, in this conversation. Let me make use of an economical ellipsis and put it this way: What do we do when Husserl says of something, 'there is no name for it'? Or when one says, as I did, perhaps

abusing the etymology, that there are two apparently contradictory significations that knit in a nominal identity, and
that at bottom there is not just one name but two names in
just one thing – and the speculative *chance* [chance, luck,
fortune] of this name, Hegel would say, is that in a single
name there are two names, and therefore there is no name,
because when one says that a name is two names there is *no
name* – what do we do then? What does one do when one
says that there is no name for it? Is something being designated that is beyond the nameable, that is unnameable?

I think a more complicated gesture is being performed:
one names that for which there is no name; and one names
in fact, each time, the possibility of the name. There is no
name for the possibility of the name, but one names the
possibility of the name; which means, getting back to the
example of iterability with its twin aspects of repetition of
the same and affirmation of the new, that here I name the
possibility of the name. Every time there is a name – by which
we mean proper name – the word can remain the same
while naming something new each time. The very possibility
of the name is iterability: the possibility of repeating the
same, but each time to name an other or to name the same
otherwise. It is with the same word that I designate the
same in a new way each time. To put it another way, naming itself would be impossible without iterability. Taking
the case of Socrates, since we mentioned it a moment ago:
the name Socrates has to remain the same, the same has to
be repeated, but each time I say 'Socrates' the naming has
to be another and to designate the same otherwise and as
something other. So in naming, in nameability itself, there is
iterability, or what has no name.

When Husserl says, for example, 'there is no name for it',
he is referring as much to the name as to that for which
there is no name. He is saying something about the name,
namely: What is a name? Husserl, here, would appear to
know what a name is, and so he says: for this flux of absolute
subjectivity there is no name; the possibility of naming the
name is not nameable. When Husserl says 'there is no name
for it', he says: given the structure of the philosophical lexicon

and grammar, the appropriate word cannot be found, and every name is a betrayal because it stabilizes and spatializes the flux. Language is by definition incapable of defining this becoming. Husserl gives us a thesis on the name, on what in language, in a certain Western grammar, bears the name of name, i.e., the repetitive fixity of an appellation that, in short, *stabilizes*: it does not move. It is this structure that is in question when one says: there is no name for it.

Ferraris.   The historian always thinks that his contemporary the theoretician is ingenuous, that he's under an illusion. I think he's right.

Derrida.   Philosophical gestures that consist in saying, 'we are going to begin, we are going back to square one, we are going to start from scratch' – as Descartes does, as Kant does in one way and Husserl in another – all vindicate ingenuousness, but they are ingenuous themselves, and ingenuously so. They claim to recover the *archē*, the beginning, and are thus naive; but they are more naive than they wish to be – if I may put it that way – since they believe it is possible to be naive. Naivety consists in believing that one can be naive – that one can begin at birth, as if one had just been born (naive [*naïf*] in fact means that 'one has just been born' [*on vient de naître*]). This declared ingenuousness conceals a deeper one, which consists in believing that one can begin, when instead it has *already* begun.

When I say 'I am ingenuous', this is in a way both more modest and more cunning than the attitude we've just spoken of. More cunning, because I try to take into account the fact that one has to be too ingenuous to believe it possible to be ingenuous – and here we have the basis of the deconstructive critique of all claims to an absolute beginning in philosophy. And more modest, because in fact (and here it is sufficient to go back to what we said earlier about opening to the other) one is faced with something [a]new [*de nouveau*]; I am always faced with something [a]new. I know that philosophically it is naive to believe it possible to be naive, yet at the same time it is absolutely new each time. For example, in this conversation of ours I would not have found the energy to speak if I weren't speaking with you, in a singular situation, anew, with a feeling of absolute freshness, *the sea on my right* . . . And here I am, disarmed, I have to start all over again, to expose myself to the newness of the thing, to the surprise; really, I feel like an absolute beginner, ingenuous, having to face up to the surprise that comes from the other. And that's how it is in the face of each text. Thus it is *also* without cunning that I declare my ingenuousness, because I find it for the first time; and then I know, on the basis of the memory I have cultivated – if you will – as a philosopher and historian of philosophy, that faced with the infinite task of beginning anew one is always ingenuous, at any age, in any culture. No repetition will ever exhaust the novelty of what comes. Even if one were able to imagine the contents of experience wholly repeated – always the same thing, the same person, the same land-scape, the same place and the same text returning – the fact that the present is new would be enough to change every-thing. Temporalization itself makes it impossible not to be ingenuous in relation to time.

Ferraris. And also in relation to place. It is perfectly nat-ural for identical twins not to have exactly the same char-acter: A sees B, B sees A, so they absolutely do not see the same thing.

Derrida. This is true of everything that is dual. Imagine a couple, in the ecstasy of infinite love – it is infinite differ-ence: the eyes meet, and what the one sees is absolutely other than what the other sees. Likewise in harmony, in the most sympathetic, symbiotic and symphonic accord. What I see at this moment has no relation to what you see, and we understand each other: you understand what I'm saying to you, and for that to happen it is necessary, really necessary, that what you have facing you should have no relation, no commensurability, with what I myself see facing you. And it is this infinite difference that makes us always ingenuous, always absolutely new. Call it monadology – the fact that between my monad – the world as it appears to me – and yours, no relation is possible: hence the hypothesis of God, who thinks of compossibility, pre-established harmony, etc. But from monad to monad, and even when monads speak to one another, there is no relation, no passage. The translation totally changes the text. From this point of view, it is a question for me of a Leibnizianism without God, so to speak: which means that, *nevertheless*, in these monads, in this hypersolipsism, the appeal of God finds place; God sees from your side and from mine at once, as absolute third; and so *there* where he is not there, he is there; *there* where he is not there, is his place.

Naples, 25 May 1994

V

Ferraris. In *The Concept of Mind*, Ryle writes that a witness
is not essentially a witness because he remembers something
but because he witnessed it. You, on the contrary, maintain
that witnessing depends above all on remembering. The perception and the mirage of authenticity give way to idealization, iterability, the technical.

Derrida. Because the *stigmē* – the point of the instant
apparently required by testimony as pure presence, singular,
irreplaceable and unique – not only is divided, but *has to*
divide and repeat itself, authenticity is exposed to the technical [*la technique*]. Here, however, the technical is not a
threat to authenticity, not a negative accident, but rather
the condition of the effect of authenticity. If I were unable
to repeat my testimony, and if consequently there were no
iterability to broach/breach [*entamer*] or divide the instant,
there would be no truth either, the testimony would have
no value. Even the value of authenticity is guaranteed as far
as possible by what would appear to threaten it, namely
repetition, and as soon as there is repetition there is the
possibility of technicization, and thus of registration, archiv-
ization and idealization.

The relations between what you call authenticity and the
technical are extremely paradoxical, because, contrary to what
one might think, they are reciprocal possibilities and at the
same time, of course, a reciprocal danger; since authenticity
depends on iterability, iterability threatens what it at the

same time makes possible. This is why it can never be proved
that testimony is authentic. There is no way of proving a lie
or a truth. If someone tells you, 'I did not lie, I said something that is not true, but I did not lie, I had no lying
intention, I gave testimony that is false but not false testimony', you can never prove the contrary because it all took
place within himself and so is a question of faith, and inten-
tionality. You cannot give proof of a lie. You can give proof
of a non-truth or error, but not of a false testimony. And
this has to do with what we have just said about authenticity and iterability.

There is, of course, the theme of the *individuum*, ineffab-
ility – that is one aspect; but here it is a question of the
fact that I cannot put myself in someone else's place, I
cannot – as Husserl would put it – have any intuitive access
to another's intention. The idea of testimony requires
exemplarity, and that means absolute singularity: a testimony takes place *once* on the subject of what takes place
once, the testimony is unique, irreplaceable – it is the logic
of the instant. But this uniqueness must immediately be
opposed to its contrary – I have to be replaceable in the
very place where I am irreplaceable. When I say 'I'm telling
you the truth about what I saw there', it means: (1) anyone
whosoever in my place would have seen the same thing,
that's why what I say is true; (2) I'm ready to repeat univer-
sally and infinitely this statement that is unique, but that
becomes ideal – and so all of a sudden the unique becomes
universal, universalizable. The schema of exemplarity presup-
poses testimony. In Kant's *Metaphysics of Morals*, my respect
for the other is a respect for someone who is an example of
obedience to the law; I respect the other person as unique,
but at the same time she is an example of a finite being who
obeys the law, and respect is owed to the law. I want to
emphasize that the question of the example is in this sense
intimately bound up with moral law, as is testimony.

This is, moreover, what is paradoxical in the question of
testimony in its relation to the event. Testimony implies
that something happens [*arrive*], and that this happening
[*arrivée*] is irreducible; but at the same time, insofar as it is

exemplary and thus universalizable, what is exemplary no longer even needs an event. The text of Blanchot's that I read yesterday is anchored in the real, they are things that really happened to him, but at the same time everything he says about survival, about death, could also be said without its having happened: the event somehow served to illustrate a structure.[3] Everything Heidegger writes about the relation to death as possibility of the impossible is described by Blanchot in that story. In a way, it is not necessary to have faced a firing squad (and survived) to think and to say the possibility of the impossible. And yet *there was testimony*, because there was a dated event. But this event is a non-event; in this event, Blanchot tells us that, ultimately, nothing happened.

I reproached myself for not having posed the question yesterday of the status of Blanchot's text. Is it literature or not? The story can be considered as the narration of a real event, that happened to Maurice Blanchot, or else as a literary fiction. Some people may say it is not true, that the author imagined something that *could* have happened to him. But then, who is to say? One does not know whether the text is testimony or fiction. The text, even in the way it is written, mimics fiction. Blanchot is the author of a text but there is no guaranteed identity between Blanchot and the narrator. Even so, one still has to distinguish various moments within the text. In the last paragraph, when he says that later on he encountered Malraux, one has the impression that this may be Maurice Blanchot.

Ferraris.   Malraux can't prove us wrong.

---

[3]   Derrida is referring to the inaugural session of his seminar at the Ecole des Hautes Etudes en Sciences Sociales for the academic year 1994–5, which took place the previous day. During the lecture he discussed a passage from Maurice Blanchot's text *L'Instant de ma mort*, describing the 'testimony' of a young French Resistance fighter facing a Nazi firing squad in 1944, up to 'the instant of my death'. A transcription of the session was published in the Italian edition of this book, but has been omitted here. An expanded version of the lecture has been published in Maurice Blanchot / Jacques Derrida, *The Instant of my Death / Demeure: Fiction and Testimony*, trans. Elizabeth Rottenberg, Stanford, CA: Stanford University Press, 2000 [Eds].

Derrida. Neither Malraux, nor anyone else. It's a secret.

Ferraris. In 1968 you wrote that the 'différance' that makes presentation possible is never presented as such. The same could be said about the schematism in Kant, as possibility of the sensibilization of the insensible, and thus, as we have said, as secret.

Derrida. There's no question, difference is not presented, or nature loves to hide. But such hiding is not the only secret. The professional secret, confessional secret, military secret, political secret, the secret police, the secret in novels, etc., all the semantics of the secret are possibilities that are more determinate than the general possibility to which you refer. I would particularly insist on the political, on the public and private regions; the secret is not reducible to the private, but what should the political, what should democracy do with the possibility of the secret? In *The Politics of Friendship* I included some texts of Kant's on the secret, on the secret a priori, but also on the conscious secret and on keeping the secret. I have attempted, in my seminar, to link this secret with the unconscious, censorship, etc.

Now, I do not privilege the schematism as any more than one example among others; it is not unusual to find third terms, mixed terms, intermediaries, which participate in the two terms of an opposition at the same time – sensible and intelligible, for example – putting the opposition in check. There are other examples of this in the history of philosophy. It is true of the imagination in general. But all third terms, all undecidables respect this logic. Of course the case of Kant is particularly interesting, on account of the huge role the 'third' plays from the viewpoint of time, and of the relation passivity–activity.

Ferraris. From Herder on, and throughout the period (which in part is still our own) of the 'linguistic turn', it has been said that the schematism (and in general the 'triality' it incarnates) is language. This seems to me an abuse and an impoverishment. Augustine, in *De Trinitate* (XV, 10, 18), says that 'outside' there is language and sight, but 'inside', when we think, they are the same thing. It is the experience of remembering Carthage that we have placed in our exergue.

Derrida. The first step for me, in the approach to what I proposed to call deconstruction, was a putting into question of the authority of linguistics, of logocentrism. And this, accordingly, was a protest against the 'linguistic turn', which, under the name of structuralism, was already well on its way. The irony – painful, at times – of the story is that often, especially in the United States, because I wrote 'il n'y a pas de hors-texte' [there is nothing outside the text], because I deployed a thought of the 'trace', some people believed they could interpret this as a thought of language (it is exactly the opposite). Deconstruction was inscribed in the 'linguistic turn', when it was in fact a protest against linguistics! And that gave rise to a great many misunderstandings, not only in philosophy and literary criticism, but also in history – there are some historians, epistemologists of history (Clifford Geertz, Hayden White, etc.), who have attempted to apply the linguistic turn to history. And their work has been placed in the same camp as mine – quite wrongly, in my opinion. Though it may well be true that I have more of an affinity with them than with more classical historians. Nevertheless, I do the best I can to mark the limits of the linguistic and the limits of the rhetorical – this was the crux of my profound debate with Paul de Man, who had a more 'rhetoricist' interpretation of deconstruction.

As you know, I take great interest in questions of language and rhetoric, and I think they deserve enormous considera-tion; but there is a point where the authority of final juris-diction is neither rhetorical nor linguistic, nor even discursive. The notion of trace or of text is introduced to mark the limits of the linguistic turn. This is one more reason why I prefer to speak of 'mark' rather than of language. In the first place the mark is not anthropological; it is prelinguistic; it is the possibility of language, and it is everywhere there is relation to another thing or relation to an other. For such relations, the mark has no need of language.

When I began to use the word 'logocentrism' and to make it a theme of deconstruction, I was not thinking of the *logos* itself, but rather – given the period in which I was writing – of the centrism of language in general – of discourse – in structuralism. Later the thing was extended to designate not the authority or privilege of the *logos* itself, but of a certain interpretation of the *logos*. And from this point of view, if you will, logocentrism is something very Western, while there is a phonocentrism in practically all writing and especially in the relation, in the interpretation of the relation between speech and writing. In all writing in general. The authority of speech can be found at a certain point within every culture in general, as an economic phase of humanization, while logocentrism is linked not only to speech but, in the West – in the Greek West – to the authority of the *logos*. The paradox is that, even though I proposed to deconstruct the hegemony of linguistics, my work is often presented as a linguisticism. That said, you're quite right, the centre – if there is one – is not *there*.

The analysis of idealization, which, with iterability, makes it possible to disincarnate the sensible individual, and which I use as a deconstructive concept, is itself at work in the concept of *eidos*. *Eidos*, in Greek, is in the first place a sensible figure, a sensible contour, a form, and it comes to mean a figure that is not sensible. There is a process that may be called metaphorization – idealization – within the *eidos* itself. It may be interpreted Platonically or not, but when one uses the word 'idealization' one continues to draw on the locus where what we hold to be deconstructible is constituted, namely the *eidos* or the idealism of the *eidos*, or the privilege of sight – metaphorical sight – or the privilege of objectivity. The paradox of this concept of idealization, as I make use of it within a deconstructive process, is that it is borrowed in some way from a sort of Platonism that, from Plato to Husserl, privileges the form of sensible–insensible or insensibilized intuition.

Paris, 10 November 1994

VI

Vattimo. When I write an essay on my own, I can also justify myself – they called me, they asked me for an article. But when working with others, as we are doing now for example, the problem arises of what you imagine you're doing and why you're doing it. The book we did together in Capri on 'Religion', to give another example, stemmed from a publishing initiative, but there was a break between the publisher's economic and practical idea and the choice of the theme.[4] Why is one theme chosen rather than another, especially in a group project? It is a question that reflects retrospectively upon the justification of individual work, and upon that of the work of others. The curiosity I have always had about your work is this: what about – what has become of – certain important justifications, referring to the circumstances and the time, that you advanced at the beginning of *Of Grammatology*? And, conversely, can deconstruction be the work of a collective, or is it rather – as in fact is often said – an individual activity, literary or creative?

Derrida. This question surprises me a little and yet I find it necessary. I shall attempt to knot two threads. The first is that I try to place myself, or I find myself placed, before the question: what is going on today [*qu'est-ce qui se passe*], what is happening [*qu'est-ce qui arrive*]? If I am to speak and

---

4 J. Derrida and G. Vattimo (eds), *Religion* (Cambridge: Polity 1998).

write publicly, I have to take into account the singular and distinctive happenings of today. Let's take religion as an example, a huge and extremely old question, whose infinite richness overflows us at every instant – it fills and overflows the libraries of the whole world. It cannot be tackled seriously, especially in the course of a two-day meeting between friends [Capri, 28 February–1 March 1994]. Nevertheless, I had the feeling that – despite the enormous tradition going back thousands of years – something singular is happening today, of which there are a great many signs in the world. Something completely new, to which we have to respond and with respect to which we have to situate ourselves. And it occurred to me that, to get to grips with our here and now, with what is original in our 'historical' situation, religion is not the worst guiding thread.

Now for the second thread. Let me try to respond to the second part of your question, where you said: 'People say that basically your way of writing is a bit peculiar, that you have aesthetic or poetic concerns, etc.' I do have concerns that may be called 'aesthetic' – I don't particularly like that word; I have a concern about composition, about form, whose origin is not, however, exclusively aesthetic. Faced with the singularity of the world event, I have to respond to it singularly, with my signature, in my own way, not as an aesthetic fetish, but to take a responsibility. It happens to me [*ça m'arrive*] and I have to respond, me, with my language, my age, my history, my *ductus*, my way of writing, of making the letters, even if it is illegible. Naturally one has to invent, not in the sense of fiction but in that of the performative: here is my response to a given situation; if it is a signature, then it too has to be an event, in its way, modestly, but it has to have the form of something that is not simply constative – it too, like all acts of responsibility, has to pledge itself, to give as a pledge. This is how I would explain my concern about writing, form, rhetoric, politics. To be sure, mine is not only a concern with responsibility in the noble ethico-metaphysical or ethico-juridical sense, it is also a concern about testimony, about testament, about leaving something that has a certain form, that appears. The big question is (the question of beauty, and I cannot tackle it so fast. I want this responsibility and this signature to have a certain form – but what guides me in the structuring of this form? It's hard to say. But it is true that the concern for composition has a relation with the proper name, with one's manner of dressing and appearing. One wants it to have that form, *voilà*. I don't know whether I would call this 'aesthetic', because I don't know very well, in this case, what that means; it has to do with desire, beauty, sex and death.

Vattimo.   The traditional distinction between philosophy and poetry is based on the fact that poetry gives no preliminary justifications. Heidegger, when he begins *Being and Time*, sets before us the question of the oblivion of Being, justifying it on the basis of a quotation from Plato, intended as the index of a 'description' of the overall situation. The reply regarding form is the second thread, but it is the first thread that counts, i.e. the fact that there is something that happens. According to a traditional philosophical reply, one justifies the point of departure on the basis of a situation; then the treatment of the question becomes descriptive, taking the form of the most faithful description possible of the structure of Being, so that people may conform to it. But the notion of reply – in your perspective and perhaps in the one in which all of us are – can no longer justify itself in terms of adequacy and adequation.

Derrida.   I ought to have specified that what happens deconstructs itself in the process. It is not I who deconstruct; rather, something I call 'deconstruction' happens to the experience of a world, a culture, a philosophic tradition: 'it' deconstructs, *ça ne va pas*, there is something that budges, that is in the process of being dislocated, disjointed, disadjoined, and of which I begin to be aware. Something is 'deconstructing' and it has to be answered for. In beginning *Of Grammatology* I set out from a sort of observation: today language is no longer a region, it has won the totality of space, its reign now has a sort of extension without limits; and, simultaneously, language becomes writing, with an invasion

of the graphic structure of experience. I gave a certain number
of examples of all this, in current life, in political life, in
genetics, in telecommunications, a sort of photograph, an
image of the world and of a world in the process of changing, and thus of 'deconstructing'.

Many of my texts may give the impression of beginning
without preliminary justification, without that still classic
moment which you described in Heidegger. I would say it is
an appearance that depends on an elliptic economy. As I write
in principle for a highly restricted community of readers who
I presume share a philosophical culture with me, I say to
myself, also out of modesty: I'm not going to start all over
again, I'm not going to open my text as *The Critique of Pure
Reason* or *Being and Time* opens. That said, I am also convinced that it is no longer possible to write a great philosophical 'machine'. At least, I myself am not able to. I always
operate through small oblique essays. Heidegger abandoned
Being and Time, and never wrote any more books. I think
the form of the systematic, encyclopedic or circular book is
impossible; and in *Of Grammatology* I start off by saying:
that's it, no more books.

Your question is perhaps that of the introduction, the
preface, the overture. In the 'Outwork' ['Hors-livre'] of
Dissemination I attempt to tackle the question systematically and, beginning with Hegel, to mark all the aporias of
such introductions and circularity. This is what seems to be
in the process of deconstruction.

Vattimo. You have justified the lack of a general and
Hegelian vision in two ways that are complementary, but
perhaps also contradictory: on the one hand, 'I suppose one
already knows it'; on the other, 'I think it's no longer possible'. If the first answer is the right one, one might wonder if
anything has changed since *Of Grammatology*, and how you
would repeat or summarize it today. If it's the second, you
will say, perhaps, that it was the last general gaze that justified the fact that no further general gaze is possible. We can
always say that some questions have no answer, but then
we'd be in the situation of the man who writes to the Pope

and then publishes an 'epistolarium' consisting of no letters but his own, since the Pope never answered him.

Derrida.   Even within this microcommunity for which we write, I think that very few people share the same views; but still, even if they were extremely rare, if there were only one or two – and here we are already approaching the question of community and friendship – I would base myself on them, I think they have to be the basis, for reasons not of aristocracy but of economy: for the sake of formalization and rapidity. But then again, these shared views had little to do with my own work and the people who read me, I was writing about world culture and what is happening in the world today. I don't think there really are two types of text, *Of Grammatology* and the others. Each text begins differently, it is a compromise between the rhetoric of a classical introduction and another kind of invention.

Your second observation leaves me considerably more disarmed, and I must confess that I cannot answer the question: Why deconstruct? To what end deconstruct? If deconstruction is anything but an initiative of my own, or a method, or a technique, but is what happens, the event one takes note of, then why go in that direction? Why make the situation worse? Should it be remedied? Should it be reconstructed? If – as a hypothesis – there is a minimal duty, it is the duty to be lucid, the duty not to miss what happens. But this experience is not sufficient, one has to know if one is *for* or *against*, if one is happy about it or not, and if one wishes to accentuate the process or slow it down. It is here that I have no answer.

Of course I do not want the performative gesture, the signature, the initiative I take, to be too anachronistic. So I have to be in tune with what is going on, even if being of one's time means, here, being attuned to something that in itself is anachronistic. Deconstruction is anachronism in synchronism, it is a manner of attuning to something that is out of joint and out of tune. One has to attune, but it is also a question of doing otherwise, and of inviting others to do something by saying: Here's what I think one has to do. Here I have nothing but experiences of aporia, which I think must not be forgotten – I think they have to be taken seriously. But I have no contents to propose. I must have had occasion to say, for example, that it's better that there be a future [de l'avenir], and that I move in the direction of deconstruction because it is what comes [qui vient], and it's better that there be a future, rather than nothing. For something to come there has to be a future, and thus *if there is* a categorical imperative, it consists in doing everything for the future to remain open. I am strongly tempted to say this, but then – in the name of what would the future be worth more than the past? More than repetition? Why would the event be preferable to the non-event? Here I might find something that resembles an ethical dimension, because the future is the opening in which the other happens [arrive], and it is the value of the other or of alterity that, ultimately, would be the justification. Ultimately, this is my way of interpreting the messianic. The other may come, or he may not. I don't want to programme him, but rather to leave a place for him to come if he comes. It is the ethic of hospitality.

You said that at least Heidegger, when he speaks of the oblivion of Being, says 'one must not forget Being'; and that at bottom this is what justifies, accounts for, gives rise to his entire discourse. Yes and no: he does say that, but he also says the opposite – namely, that there is no question of remembering Being without oblivion; therefore it cannot be said that Heidegger made the memory of Being into a sort of imperative of final jurisdiction.

Vattimo. I would just say that what Heidegger wants is that we not forget the oblivion, i.e. that we not forget that the memory of Being is a memory of facts we have forgotten, and that Being cannot but be forgotten. That's something anyway. But your point is well taken. I think that opening to the other, letting the other happen, could also be interpreted, by a 'weak thought' philosopher like myself, in the sense that the other is always better than I am. To say it like that, in general, is perhaps self-calumnious, but why should I make room for the other, if not because the imperative that is still deeper, still more categorical, is an ecstatic imperative, of 'excessus sui'? It is the question of friendship and community, and, again, of the microcommunity of readers: I am not the bearer of a universal reason on the basis of which I justify the fact of speaking of one thing rather than another, but neither do I speak only in the name of my punctual individuality. Rather, I recognize a sort of affinity. Pareyson, my teacher, whose old office we are in right now, put it in terms of congeniality. Why do I prefer to interpret certain works, certain authors, rather than others? There is no justification, but there is congeniality.

Derrida. 'Leaving room for the other' does not mean 'I have to make room for the other'. The other is in me before me: the ego (even the collective ego) implies alterity as its own condition. There is no 'I' that ethically makes room for the other, but rather an 'I' that is structured by the alterity within it, an 'I' that is itself in a state of self-deconstruction, of dislocation. This is why I hesitated just now to use the word 'ethical'. This gesture is the possibility of the ethical but is not simply the ethical, which is why I speak of the messianic: the other is there in any case, it will arrive if it wants, but before me, before I could have foreseen it.

Recently I was on the examining board of a thesis defence, where the candidate attempted to show – against Heidegger, who said that Hegel was passé – that Hegel had a future [*avenir*]. In trying to reconstruct, in Hegel and in philosophic tradition, the possibility of the relation to the future [*à l'avenir*], she used the French expression '*voir venir*': for there to be an anticipation, an ecstasy, one has to *voir venir* [wait and see]. In the discussion, I tried to show that, for there to be a future as such – which means surprise, alterity – one must no longer *voir venir*, there must not even be a horizon of anticipation, a horizon of waiting. And thus the fact that the future rushes onto me, comes onto me, precisely where I don't even expect it, don't anticipate it, don't 'see it coming', means that the other is there before me, that it comes before [*prévient*], precedes and anticipates me. The other is not even simply the future [*futur*], it is, so to speak, the anterior future [*l'avenir avant*], the advance on the future [*avenir*]. Which means that I am not proprietor of my 'I', I am not proprietor of the place open to hospitality. Whoever gives hospitality ought to know that he is not even proprietor of what he would appear to give. The case of the signature is analogous: usually interpreted as one's very own mark, it is instead what I cannot appropriate, cannot make my own.

My signature is the moment of highest responsibility in a deep irresponsibility. When I say that, basically, I write for those with whom I share a language, culture, place, home, it is not a question of 'belonging' to communities, of property or ownership, because I would say about language what I have just said about the signature. French, for example, is 'my' language, I have no others, but at the same time it is radically foreign to me – it does not 'belong' to me, it is not my property. It is to this extent that 'I have my' idiom. Place, family, language, culture, are not my own, there are no places that 'belong'. I do not want to deny the fact that I talk, all the time, about something that does resemble a 'belonging'; I know perfectly well that I write on the basis of my age, culture, family, language, but my relation to these seemingly communal structures is one of expropriation, of disownership. I no more belong to these things than they belong to me; my point of departure is there where this belonging has broken. It's like we said at the beginning: my point of departure is what happens, but insofar as it is in the process of deconstructing. I don't know the nuance of the word 'congeniality' in Italian, but what would frighten me in the word is something that acknowledges naturality and birth, 'genius'. *Politics of Friendship* is a book not altogether in favour of fraternity – that so very powerful motif, Christian, revolutionary, and universal all at once, which is always linked to birth, soil, blood.

Vattimo.   Pareyson read Goethe a great deal, so there was a somewhat biologistic component. But it's more complicated than that. We are here because we've read your texts among others, and we've found them more interesting than those of Searle, for example.

Derrida. I do not believe that a philosophical community exists in the world today. If one insisted on affirming that there is indeed such a community, even if its members do not agree with or do not understand one another, then I would say that, yes, there are people who do indeed share this situation of absolute misunderstanding, who know that under the name of philosophy they discourse in ways that cannot be translated into one another. If a reporter from CNN asks me such a question at seven in the morning, that's my answer. If I am asked the question in other circumstances – for example here, today – I think we could get very far with the analysis of what we have in common, despite our differences, misunderstandings or idioms. And my answer would not be the same if I were talking about what the three of us have in common, for example, or a group of philosophers in Turin who will be meeting this evening.[5] Or, of course, if I were answering the question in England or Germany. We have in common among other things – just to state the most evident – a German, Nietzschean, Heideggerian, phenomenological, hermeneutical culture, an attention to what is going on in the contemporary world. This is a sort of capital, so to speak, that we draw on all the time, and that makes it possible for us to understand one another, but that is the common capital of a very small number of people. Why, I wonder, are these few people, today, in Italy, in France, in Europe, in spite of not being widely read, still not totally ignored?

Vattimo. I shall be introducing you this evening. I shall begin – following your own lead – by saying that we all have a long-standing affinity with these themes, since we all come from the same family, etc. That's not too bad, but it's like explaining why we went to dinner with one person instead of someone else, it is not yet a justification. I'm well aware of the fact that I'm always trying to question you from the

---

[5] Derrida, as a guest of the Institut Culturel Franco-Italien and of the Hermeneutics Department of Turin University, presented an expanded version of his 9 November 1994 lecture on Blanchot [Eds].

viewpoint of a justification of what one does, which is a question stemming from a tradition that perhaps we do not completely share. You have answered my questions. And yet it's as though you haven't given me the answer I wanted. Perhaps that is exactly what 'the other' is all about, but . . . Let's say that the problem of philosophical discourse appears to me to be the problem of a foundering foundation [*fondation défondante/fondazione sfondante*]. To respond: I speak this way because I like to, it's too short not to be too violent. At bottom, violence means slicing through a knot that, with patience, could have been untied. Violent discourse is a lack of 'discursus', i.e. of argumentation as what permits objection. That is why the foundation is demoniacal, it is silencing, while argumentation, even it makes no claim to the metaphysical value of truth, is nonetheless a friendlier attitude.

Derrida.   I'm going to answer you disarmedly. On the one hand, I do think I am capable, in certain situations, of discoursing upon the 'task of philosophy', and even of giving my discourse a certain dignity, be it ethical, political or whatever. So, to the extent that this discourse has a certain dignity, it goes beyond the present moment, and it differs radically from the reasons for which we go out to dinner together. But, on the other hand, I am absolutely desperate or sceptical, or in any case without illusions, about the grand discourse on 'the task' – not about its intrinsic value, but about what it may mean to me. I know that my life is finite – it has been finite from the start, but is now more finite than ever – that I have just a certain number of years still to live, and that everything I do is watched over, together, by death and immediate desire. For me there is no radical distinction between the grand discourse on 'the task' with all its dignity, and the reasons for wanting to go out to dinner with someone. They are not homogeneous questions, but I would not mark out a true opposition. I might make a grand discourse on 'the task' just for the immediate good it would do me, for the desire to do it, for the pleasure it would give me. Of course the desire to be with one person rather than another matters to me, but my pleasure will be all the more intense if I dine, or make love, or take a walk, with someone who will be where I am, and who will understand what I mean when I make this discourse on tasks. These two paradigms that we have treated somewhat abstractly – the grand and ambitious discourse on 'the task' and the urgencies of desire – condition one another in a way that I find, at bottom, extremely resigned, desperate . . .

Vattimo.   But also participant. I had some students who were being psychoanalysed by a Lacanian. People in psychoanalysis have a slightly detached attitude at times, they're always smiling like actors do on stage. So I was wondering – how do they get from the kitchen to the bedroom? I mean, to transform a situation just of food-making into a situation of love-making, for example. It's a verse of Rilke's that kept going round and round in my head for years, I never quite pinned it down, and until that moment I'd never understood it. Deconstruction is also a consciousness of the duplicity of situations, of the fact that there is never a total presence. In fact, if I may say so, when you were speaking about death just now I had a curiosity that I repressed: do you think about a 'survival' [afterlife] or not?

Derrida.   I think about nothing but death. I think about it all the time, ten seconds don't go by without the imminence of the thing being there. I never stop analysing the phenomenon of 'survival' as the structure of surviving, it's really the only thing that interests me, but precisely insofar as I do not believe that one lives on post mortem. And at bottom it is what commands everything – what I do, what I am, what I write, what I say.

   I do not think, however, that this thought of death, or what you referred to as detachment, disintensifies. In deconstruction there is a movement of sensitization to the multiplicity of levels of structure; at every instant, there are dislocations within the instant. But this, for me, instead of cooling and disintensifying experience, intensifies it. I don't believe there can be *full* enjoyment [*jouissance*]. If it were full it would not be an enjoyment, therefore demultiplying it does not mean a loss of intensity.

Ferraris. If one digs an abyss between aesthetics and theory or ethics (which is exactly what happens when true life is opposed to art, i.e. aesthetics in its degraded sense of figments of the imagination), one will always be reduced to giving an impoverished description, with true life on one hand, and on the other variations of the imagination that may be accepted or not, but are in any case considered essentially ornamental. But if there is in principle no difference between reality and phantasm, it is because both are a modification of a general possibility of inscription, i.e., of retention as the origin of both sensibilization and idealization.

Derrida. A word on the subject of the various figures of appearing – image, *morphē*, *eidos*, and especially phantasm. It seems to me that if, following the logic of your discourse, we take the word 'phantasm' to mean that which weaves the universal and the individual together in the image, then we come right back to what we said earlier – though we don't have time to go into it here – about the 'coming before' of the other in the I, i.e. as phantasm. But I would not free myself so easily of phantoms, as some people all too often think they do ('it's nothing but a phantom'). I think that we are structured by the phantasmic, and in particular that we have a phantasmic relation to the other, and that the phantasmicity of this relation cannot be reduced, this pre-originary intervention of the other in me.

It is here that exemplarity, universality and singularity cross each other's paths. From the very beginning of our interview we have allowed that word 'justification' to slip right in, acting as if we really knew what it meant. Now, as you know, the word is an abyss. No question, it does make reference to justice: I want my discourse to be justifiable, which is to say, just; so that I can answer for it before something we call justice, which is not, does not exist, is not a given; and then I want to respond by adjusting my discourse (a question of *fügen* and of justness), giving due consideration to what is really going on today, adjusting my discourse to historical reality, as I inherit it and as it currently deploys itself. Justification means adjusting one's discourse to history, heritage, epoch, to whatever is, but adjusting it, disadjusting it, adjusting it to what is not yet there, what is not of this world. Justification enjoins, then, that one adjust and that one disadjust in the name of justice, and that supposes, together, history and a break with history, if history means the *totality* of what is or has been.

Justification before what is not yet, before a justice that I make my appeal to or that comes, but that can not-come, is, once again, the messianic dimension, which is historical and, at the same time, has broken with history. Perhaps this value of messianicity permits us to link up with what Gianni said about the violence of 'I do it because I like to', as opposed to argumentation. I would hesitate to oppose the two. First, I am not sure that violence is an evil, and I would prefer to oppose various sorts of violence to one another rather than opposing violence to non-violence. Doing some-thing because one likes to is not simply violent and has not necessarily broken with the desire for argumentation. I know, for example, that I prefer philosophical discourse – speaking as we are now, or writing – to making political speeches from a rostrum. I have no desire to enter politics, no polit-ical ambitions; politics does interest me, and I am sometimes overtaken by dreams of being a political figure or a man of the theatre, but I know I would be very bad at it.

So I do what I like to do because I have the impression that my image is better; my image is not my own, it's the image of the other, a phantasm, for a spectator I do not even know. I have the impression that this is not simply violent, that it is a way not only of conforming to what is the best image for me, but also for the person inside or outside me that I aim to please. The modes of argumentation vary, but I don't think I argue a whit less in the most private and intimate of my experiences – there, I have the impression that, as far as I'm concerned, the deployment of argumentative power is ten times closer to the greatest possible violence, and even more developed than the power I vent in my books of philosophy.

Vattimo. I am very sensitive to this question myself and I agree for the most part with what you've said; it's just that there is also a question of different types of violence. Saying 'I affirm it because I like it' in a philosophical discussion might be one sort of violence, while saying 'I love you' in a love affair is violence of another sort. It's true, however, that one never knows where violence ends and experience begins: and the encounter, the upsetting of the reassuring homoeostasis is perhaps always a violence. But isn't deconstruction a manner of deconstructing immediacy as violence, as that to which nothing can be opposed? For example, the master is someone whose authority I recognize, someone I turn to when I want to hear the last word; but then, my work of exegesis on the master is always a manner of consuming, metabolizing, eating. I call this 'secularization'. There is always a sacred kernel, whereof I must be silent; but I always feel engaged in a secularizing, rationalizing, formalizing attitude. History would be a manner of denaturalizing fraternity, a form of cultural fraternity, because without fraternity or friendship nothing happens. But I am not obliged to have only Italian friends! My friends can also be French or American – not on the basis of the naturality you mistrust, but on the basis of a historical attitude.

Derrida. Listening to you, I was thinking about the distinction not only between different forms of violence according to the regions of discourse or of experience, but also between violence and brutality. The violence you spoke about, be it the *dressage* of animals or the very refined forms of symbolic violence in the philosophical community, for me is always the same: it is highly differentiated, but at bottom violence is irreducible, there is always *dressage, Zucht und Züchtung*. Even in the argumentation that shows the greatest respect for others there is a certain way of imprinting habits that preserves violence – a violence that cannot and must not be reduced, because otherwise there would be no more culture.

But we ought to distinguish between violence and what I am tempted to call brutality, not animality or bestiality – the brutality in a discussion, in an argumentation, the dogmatic fiat. By definition there is no natural violence, an earthquake is not violent, it is only violent insofar as it damages human interests. If we agree that there is no natural violence in the sense of naturality, then we ought to call violence that which does not let the other be what he is, does not leave room for the other. I have often been reproached, as you know, for not arguing; I find this reproach very unjust. I think, in fact, that I try never to be brutal or dogmatic, or to say: that's just how it is.

Brutality is not only an unrefined violence, it is a bad violence, impoverishing, repetitive, mechanical, that does not open the future, does not leave room for the other. And it is clear that brutality also has an aesthetic connotation, even if I do not wish to give the aesthetic dimension final jurisdiction here. Nevertheless, it's true that brutality reduces to the amorphous, impoverishes form, leads to a loss of differentiation. Perhaps this is all a slightly Apollonian manner of defending against orgiastic, or Dionysian, violence, which can play on the formless, the amorphous, fusion, but if difference is violence and violence is differentiating, brutality homogenizes and effaces singularity.

Turin, 19 January 1995

What is There?

Maurizio Ferraris

I

1. Index

Ontology has wrongly been considered a science of scarcity when in fact, from Clauberg on, it has been a science of abundance. In this sense Quine is perfectly right when, in the first essay ['On What There Is'] of *From a Logical Point of View*, to the question he poses – 'What is there?' – he answers, with untroubled irony, 'Everything'. But troubles start right away, as soon as one attempts to distinguish the different cases implied by such an ecumenical reply. What is there, then? There is for example *this* body, *this* sheet of paper, *this* fire. A finger, generally the index, gives a sign towards something, and indicates it as *this*. And this is *presence*, ontology in the simple and hyperbolic sense. Here we have a primary *phainesthai*, which we would be inclined to name 'presence' in the proper sense – proper as opposed to metaphorical – if it were not for the fact that, as in the *Meditations on First Philosophy*, there is first of all a *cogito* with respect to which body, sheet, fire are present (and whose presence is exposed to hyperbolical doubt). This consideration opens a crack (Kant called it the true scandal of philosophy) in the most ancient conviction of philosophy and common sense; the *kritērion tēs alētheias* according to which all sensations are true. All at once everything is turned upside down, just as when, in Husserl's example, the man I was looking at in the shop window shows itself to be a mannequin. By the same token, precisely that which is *not* seen, the *cogito*, presents itself as the only indubitable presence, so that in order to say *this* body, and ultimately also *this cogito*, which is mine, I will have to submit it to a mixed analysis of intuition and reasoning (i.e. of blind or deferred intuition). Such analysis, revealing the *cogito* to be finite, makes it possible to postulate an omnipotent, existing and veracious infinite, conquering the hyperbolic doubt that was beginning to undermine even the certainty of the *cogito* (which, in its presumption of existence, could also have been nothing more than the dream of a butterfly). Ideal and not ephemeral presence is truer than sensation, which moreover appears mediated (which is why, for Strawson, interpreting Kant, outer sense, i.e. space, is more unreal than inner sense, i.e. time).

True presence thus proves to be not aesthetic but logical presence: sensation saved in its ideality. The general model of presence, based upon aesthetic presence – which one can point out, saying *this* – solidifies in logical presence, which is the 'negative' of the aesthetic one (in the Hegelian sense that the possibility that the empirico-sensible may vanish defines by opposition the perdurance of the spiritual). The ingenuous position of sense-certainty is contested. But to what extent? The situation, in fact, is complicated by the circumstance that whereas logical – unlike aesthetic – presence seems indubitable, the latter holds an extraordinary primacy, because it is precisely the *mirage* of aesthetic presence that makes us prefer logical presence. In other words (and in a formulation still largely inadequate), the logical is what guarantees presence, but the aesthetic is that upon which this guarantee models its ideal. This inversion invalidates sense-certainty and its presumption of presence, but does not undermine the *form* of that presence, which is simply saved in logic. There is no question that ideal presence does have a privilege with respect to sensible presence, as we observe when we say *'hai presente?'* [do you have present?, do you know?, do you remember?], *'ho presente'* [I have present, I know, I remember], *'tieni presente'* [hold present, bear in mind]. This does not mean, however, that the aesthetic has been cancelled; at most, it has been sublated and preserved in the logical, because, if the result of this preservation is indeed far more efficacious than the one that silently constitutes sensible presence, the fact remains that the first 'holding present' [*tener present*, bearing in mind], the model for all the others, is the one that I tacitly put into practice when I point out anything whatsoever, taking it as present. What this summary analysis suggests, then, is a chiasmus by which aesthetic presence provides the model of logical presence, which saves and protects it; but by which, at the same time, the constitutive and retentive acts of logical presence seem to mimic, at a reflective level, a certain constitution of presence in the present that posits itself as the condition of aesthetic presence itself. And making the movement even more complex is the circumstance that, in this aesthetico-logical interlacing, a thing's empirical positing is made possible – as presence, as arche-originary and apparently immediate evidence – by a system of retentions made possible by that thing itself. Specularly (later on, we shall see how this logic unfolds), a thing's simple positing is a *thesis* in the strong sense, which makes it both unique and exemplary, according to the process at work in the very common circumstance by which, in the Neo-Latin languages, pronouns such as *ipse* and *ille* gave rise to the definite articles.

It seems, then, that the aesthetic and the logical – the presence, for example, of what is indicated with a sensible finger or an intelligible one, and is seen with the eye of the body or the spirit – are determined by a *third* that regulates the transition from the one to the other. It should be noted, moreover, that this third finger or third eye seems to be *the same*; that is, it takes the form of a term superordinate to the first two, in which it participates, making them possible. What is there – what is there that is invariant (invariance being an analytical character of presence, disregarded but not contested by the varying of experience or the weakness of memory) – in logical and in aesthetic 'holding present'? We have seen what there is: not the thing, the percept or its mnestic phantasm, but rather a finger, and to be precise an index that gives a sign and says 'this', assuming it as present and in the present – as, precisely, the indicative present. This

this indicated in the present seems to be the matrix of all presence, even if we have already begun to glimpse the limits of a reference that is both defenceless and completely armoured: the presence of the index is no less problematic than everything it points to, since, as percept, the index is no less ephemeral than everything it indicates – for it may be this or that index, mine or yours, that of the right hand or the left, just as *whatever* is indicated may be *this*, and therefore *nothing* is.

The index that is saved and that rescues what it indicates is, precisely, the index as concept; i.e. as what is neither this nor that determinate index. The hand indicates with a finger, then it closes and grasps (cataleptic, i.e. comprehensible, imagination, which lends itself to prehension and comprehension, to grasping, to the *greifen* of a *Begriff*). The *this* that I indicate in the present I take and internalize, snatching it, just as a hand does, from a stay that is no longer ephemeral. This is why there are a great many hands in thought, and not sensible or ideal hands but transcendental ones, i.e., hands that are superordinate to the distinction between sensible and intelligible. This is the situation Aristotle delineates in *De Anima* 432a 2–3, where he writes that the soul is as the hand is, because in the soul, as in the hand, there is the *form* of the stone and not the stone itself (which is grasped, not embodied), so that if the hand is a tool of tools, the intellect is a form of forms and sense a form of objects of perception. It should be noted that what is said of the hand (and which can refer retrospectively to the transcendentality of the finger) holds both for *noēsis* and *aisthēsis*. Thus the constant philosophical recourse to the hand, from Descartes's 'universal' instrument in *Discourse on Method* (*Discours de la méthode*, Adam and Tannery, VI: 57), to its most pregnant formulation, in Hegel, as 'absolute' instrument (*Encyclopaedia* §411); to Heidegger's praise of the hand considered, against all evidence, as what is proper to man in *What Is Called Thinking?*, where the identification between hand and (human) thought fits in with the interpretation put forth in §6 of *Being and Time*, where Aristotle's statement that the soul is in some way all beings is held – against the Aristotelian letter – to be a specific reference to the human soul. One can well understand this recourse to a metaphor so absolute that it has been taken for the one and only *mot juste* – this recourse to a catachresis no less irreplaceable than the word 'foundation' as it is analysed by Locke, Leibniz and Kant: posited as a concept, taken and taught, the percept is here to stay. What we said earlier about the superordinate character of the hand with respect to *aisthēsis* and *noēsis* sheds further light on the question. The grasping of the sensible-insensible hand does *not at all* mean that, if the truth and future of the percept are in fact in the concept that saves *Wesen* as *Gewesen*, then the concept has done this all by itself; and, above all, does not mean that what ensured the 'change of hand' from the sensible to the intelligible was a conceptual index.

On the one hand, the index is not *immediately* the hand. The conceptual index, in fact, explains the subsumption, and thus functions only insofar as it is the part of a hand, and in no way explains the preliminary indication to grasping. On the other hand, even admitting (as we shall demonstrate) that this indicating analytically entails a grasping, the index is no more conceptual than the hand is; it is, rather, just like the sensible-intelligible hand, a function that is superordinate to both concept and percept. The concept of index, in fact, can mean two different things. In the first place, as we have seen, it may refer to an index that is not *this* or *that* index, and that as such may amount to an anatomical definition, and to a guide for the recognition of all determinate indexes. However, if an index as concept is used in order to indicate indexes as percepts, there will still be need of a 'third' index, which will not be the concept of index but, rather, a sign, the very function of indicating (which remains the same even if instead of using an index I use, for example, a rod). This absolute index, which Kant was to call the schema, is at the same time the condition of presence (be it aesthetic or logical), and would thus seem to be absolutely present. But it is as clear as day that nothing is *less* present (logically or aesthetically) than such an index. What, in fact, would be its *ti esti*? Can one really say '*this* index' as the possibility of each and every *this*? Paradoxically, only insofar as I cannot say *this* index can this help me to say *this*, according to the logic that is immanent to the schema and indeed to every form of sign – the logic by which the essence (*ousia* as sensible presence, according to the etymon of landed possession, or as intelligible possession) of the sign would consist in having no essence. In sum, while I cannot say *this* schema, in the sense that I cannot point it out (it is the difficulty Kant met, and concealed, in the concrete enumeration of the schemata), without one schema in particular (that of spatio-temporal presence) I cannot say *this* object or *this* mental state. It is the difficulty that, in the negative, presents itself (and not infrequently) when I look for the glasses I have on my nose. And the small children who, according to the obstinate superstition that holds them incapable of abstraction, look at the finger (considering it a *this*) instead of what the index is pointing to, are if anything far *more* abstract, since they produce an inflation of presences (every percept is a concept, there are no general names or ideas, and there are no indexes as signs either!). This does not mean they are incapable of signs or schemata, but if anything that they have too many of them, one for each thing, while use and habit (a passive function of memory) will bring them to reduce the – semiotic and ontological – inflation, contracting the orbit of being and making plain a certain not-being, the *me on* of the sign, which they already make use of when, looking at the finger, they take it as *this*.

2.   *Thing*

Let us shift our gaze for a moment from the index, and take a look at what it indicates. To understand *what there is* – since there is no lack of material, or so it seems – it is best to begin by following the negative way, asking ourselves *what there isn't*. There 'are not', for example, imagined things, which correspond to nothing in the world, and which thereby differ from remembered things, which once were present. 'Caesar has crossed the Rubicon' *is* in a different world from

'Caesar has drunk hemlock'; in *this* world, ours, the first Caesar is no longer, the second never was. It is true, however, that I have no difficulty imagining Caesar drinking hemlock, and that the resources I have to make use of to obtain the image I need (including the image of myself crossing the Rubicon or drinking hemlock) are no different from the ones I use to remember the streets I have to take to get home. Do we have to conclude, then, that what really 'is not' does not pertain to the fruits of a reproductive imagination but, if anything, to an imagination that is absolutely productive – an imagination without examples? In fact it is not quite so simple. Going back to a classical philosophical typology, what does it mean to say that (productive) imagination distinguishes itself from (reproductive) imagination and from sensibility because it can make us see things 'never seen'? What does it mean to be 'never seen'? That no one has ever seen it. But this *deficit* of phenomenalization has two heterogeneous values. On the one hand, I've never seen Cape Town – or, following the example of *De Trinitate*, Alexandria – (but I could very well see it); on the other, I've never seen a squared circle – or, following Russell's example, the round square cupola on Berkeley College. In the second case, the sensibilization *manqué* presents itself not as an empirical but as a transcendental defect, designating something that has not been phenomenalized due to circumstances that do not seem – at first blush – only empirical.

But is the empirical truly insignificant, or do we have to do, rather, with a transcendentalization of empirical circumstances? If nothing is more fundamental than an empirical indication, nothing is more empirical than a fundamental ontology. So, if at this point ontology appears to meet an insuperable limit, it is because *indicating* a round square cupola seems to be impossible. Look closely: what we have here is not a logical *deficit*, for when I say 'round square' I understand perfectly well what it means; to a certain extent, the difficulty may appear *logical* only because it does not appear (*non videtur*) resolvable in terms of an *aesthetic*. The round square cupola would simply extend the limits, which are strictly psychological, of the impossibility of constructing a mental image of a 'chiliagon'. There is no difficulty in understanding, and in saying, what a thousand-sided polygon is; but it is impossible to synthesize it – in its exact form – in a mental *eidos*, unless we make use of external aids, such as pencil and paper. The specific difficulty of a round square cupola consists in the fact that the limits of its figurability do not depend on the resources of an empirical psychology, but rather on the requisites of a transcendental aesthetic, for example on the fact that in *this* world, the one we point out every day, there does not exist a curved space in which there could be a round square cupola. Everyday Italian reveals itself to be quite philosophical when it uses the expression 'such a thing *does not exist*' to say that something is not possible.[1] (The expression *'non esiste'* becomes unrealistic, and 'metaphysical' in the trivial sense, when it is used to express disappointment about something happening that one hoped would not happen – 'would not be there.'[2]) It is the same argument Kant made use of to liquidate 'possible worlds': logic has nothing against telepathy (which as such is no less bizarre than *actio in distans*, whose reality, moreover, Newton had demonstrated), or the possibility that a figure be enclosed between two parallel lines; if this does not happen – says Kant – it is due to the properties of *this* world, which is, moreover, the only one we can *point out*.

In all the other cases, things 'never seen' are things that might be seen (Trendelenburg alludes to this when, against Kant, he maintains that the distinction between analytical and synthetic is psychological), and that result from things that have been seen. Whether those things exist or not is a question not of gnoseology but, once again, of ontology: I shall never see Caesar, but this depends on Caesar (or on the year in which I was born) and not on my eyes. However, from the perspective of the faculties involved, things one has never seen but that one can imagine are all on the same level. I imagine Cape Town *a little* like San Francisco (I do not know why, even if I presume it has to do with one of

---

[1] 'Take a train to the moon! *Non esiste!*' It's not possible [Eds].

[2] 'You missed your train! *Non esiste!*' What a shame! [Eds].

the faculties of the imagination discussed by Kant in §17 of the third *Critique*, and which consists not only in recalling signs of concepts after a long time, but also in reproducing the figure of an object by drawing upon many objects, of a different or of the same type). For example, I imagine a centaur by having in mind a man and a horse, or, like McX, the philosopher imagined by Quine in his synthesis of real philosophers, I think of Pegasus. But that Cape Town exists and the centaur and Pegasus do not does not mean that the imagination that thinks the centaur is more productive than the one that thinks Cape Town. Saying so would be no less absurd than concluding that there exists a device for establishing a priori the difference between perception and remembrance, or for grounding it in reason without recourse to experience. I can accompany the image with an assent, as in the *phantasia katalēptē* of Stoic phenomenology, and in this case we have remembrance; I can accompany it with scepticism, and in this case we have imagination. But the variation of consciousness upon which I found my differentiation has its court of final jurisdiction in an ontological reference: if the city I think I remember is not *that one*, then – even if subjectively I have the experience of the remembrance – 'objectively' (but the objectivity in this case is highly problematic) we have a fantasy. The inverse is also possible: I can imagine something I think does not exist; if I then discover that in fact it does exist, then what subjectively is experienced as imagination, 'objectively' may be considered as remembrance, perception or anticipation.

One might conclude from all this, then, that in order to know what there is, instead of fantasizing about possible worlds it would be better if we turned our attention to *this* one. It is on the basis of a primacy of ontology of this sort that, in the *Dioptrique* (Adam and Tannery, VI: 85), Descartes praises the philosophical value of eyeglasses, which routed the chimeras that had afflicted the fantasies of philosophers. But, once we have passed through the test of non-being, the abundance seems to be greatly reduced. One often quotes those verses of Hamlet's ('There are more things in heaven and earth, Horatio, / Than are dreamt of in your philosophy') as an affirmation of realism, which makes a fine pair with the praise of eyeglasses; but our Danish philosopher has just seen his father's ghost, and *having a vision* means a great many things that don't exactly coincide with seeing what there is. Let's take a look at some situations that, for the sake of convenience, we may call 'borderline' (although it is difficult to find a zone of experience that is intact). In what sense 'is there' a star that exploded thousands of years ago, and that we see now? Is it really there now, when we see it, when we intuitively grasp it as a phenomenon, even though per se it is no longer there? Or, more exactly, now that its being *for itself* amounts to nothing more than being *in place of itself*, the phenomenon now acting as nothing more than a reference? It is to be noted that, according to the distinction between phenomenon and noumenon, everything visible – ourselves included – could be nothing but memory and phenomenalization, no less than stars that have exploded, and appeared precisely when they have ceased to be noumena. Vice versa, if the measure of being is phenomenalization, it is problematic to say in what sense atoms, X-rays, and the sounds emitted by dog whistles *are*. To be a little more demanding, if we have assumed that there *is* only that which I indicate right now, then, with a Humean argument, it is very difficult to maintain that there *are* these books here behind me, and – at the same time – that it is only a continuous belief, given by repeated retention and by the iterability of experience, that makes me overlook these doubts.

It is probable, however, that the reader of this essay believes in my existence nearly as much as I do. We normally believe in a great many things we do not see. Take, for example, another case of telecommunication, a telephone conversation. 'Is Francesco there?' 'Yes, he's here.' In this case, I can speak to him without him being physically present and, except for a series of variations that, moreover, are not adiaphorous, such as the simultaneity that reinforces the effect of presence, it is as if I were writing to him. It is typical that here a scriptural horizon does not so much replace as, rather – according to the chiasmus we sketched in the previous section – make possible a logical presence as deferral of aesthetic presence. This becomes clearer in the case where one answers, 'No, he isn't here'. The fact that Francesco isn't at home does not mean that he's never existed (even if this ought to be Parmenides' conclusion, and that of the Neo-Parmenideans with him). I retain an image of Francesco, I've seen him on other occasions, I presume that he was born, and it is thus on the basis of an internal writing (retention, memory) that I expect a presence (conjectural, for that matter; in this case, telephonic). In a certain way, this retention orients me in the expectation of an aesthetic presence. The same thing happens – and its scriptural character is even clearer – when I come up against an answering machine – 'We're not here'. It is likely that they aren't there, but I know they *were* there and that probably they *will be* there (will be back), and I am not set on finding dishonesty or contradiction in the fact that when they *were there*, recording the message, they said they *were not there*.

This being and not being, not by chance, is the characteristic form of time as it has been analysed from Aristotle to Augustine to Hegel. How can something be and not be? Apart from the paucity of the cases we have examined, which moreover call for phenomenological refinement, because they represent scenes of writing in a telecommunicative context that, in turn, offers itself as a scriptural frame, we have to take note of a minimal structure. That which makes me believe Francesco to be present, even if he's not here in front of me, and keeps me from concluding that he's never existed when they answer that he isn't there, is the time with which I am constructing my experience. If a voice – speech – is present, it is because it is *in* the present. But the paradox is that what makes presence possible vanishes in the very thing it makes present, and I no longer take account of time when Francesco is there, while, when they answer that he's not there, I begin to take account of it once more, I assume he is not present because he's not there in the present. The ontological fleetingness of speech is transformed, in a successful communicative act, into a presence while, if I wish to do the experiment the other way round, seeking to measure time with the canons of the presence it made possible, I find myself in the situation of having to conclude that time *et est et non est*, because: 'If no one asks me, I know; if I want to explain it to someone who does ask me, I do not know' (*The Confessions of St Augustine*, XI, 14.17). As Plotinus puts it in the first *Ennead*, consciousness obscures what it makes possible. In sum, in saying 'there is still time' and, even more, 'there is no more time', one is making intimately paradoxical affirmations, because they affirm or deny the being of something that, as such, seems to be without it.

But it should be noted here that these characteristics are the same as the index: if I take the index as a thing, it is not; but if I take it as a reference it is not either, precisely because, as reference, it has no being in itself. The index is a certain not-being-there [*non esserci*] that posits itself as the condition of being-there [*esserci*] – the not-being-there of indication and of the present as the possibility of the aesthetic presence that, in turn, acts as a model also for the logical presence that surpasses and hoards it as it negates it. But this very fleetingness entails a distinctive asthenia of the presence that not-being-there has made possible, which is reflected in the circumstance that brought Augustine (*Contra Faustum*, XII, 6) to say that matter, too, *et est et non est*. In doing so, the Christian philosopher repeats the *Timaeus*: it is wrong to say 'this' fire, since 'this' is only that which remains identical in all the forms taken by fire or by water. And yet on the basis of this dual fleetingness, of time and of the presence time has made possible, the 'this' maintains its unlimited sovereignty. Perhaps because indication already, from the outset, reaches out towards grasping. At the beginning of the *Philosophical Investigations* Wittgenstein condemns Augustine's philosophy of language, precisely because Augustine ascribes the learning of words to ostension. But the Augustinian position is, in some way, inevitable. It is true that Augustine does not describe the functioning of language correctly, because he is in fact explaining how a language (in this case, the first language) is learned; now, this learning process is, rather, one of writing, so Augustine is quite right to draw our attention not to the words but to the finger that produces the ostension. And yet, when Wittgenstein, later on (§§385ff), asks himself whether it is possible 'for someone to learn to do sums in his head without ever doing written or oral ones', he repeats exactly the hypothesis for which every event, be it aesthetic or logical, has its origin in the possibility of retention, *whose first form will be the ostension ensured by the finger*. Through a process we shall attempt to specify, but whose outlines can already be glimpsed, give someone a finger and they will take the whole hand – so to speak. When I say *'immantinente'* it is as if I said *'seduta stante'*:[3] these expressions produce a coded extension of the present or of the this, which are stopped in their tracks, as in the Biblical miracle where Joshua asked God to stop the course of the sun. But isn't our miracle banal? When Aristotle writes, in the *De Memoria* (449b 31–450a 5), that thinking is like drawing a figure, he explicitly draws our attention to the fact that it is not a question of using images in thought (for, indeed, that which is drawn is great or small, i.e. determined, unlike that which is referred to in thinking), but rather of showing how thought is made possible by a sum of retentions. Now, as regards sensation the situation is the same: according to the argument of the *De Anima* (431a 14–15), for the dianoetic soul *phantasmata* act as *aisthēmata*. But these *aisthēmata* are no less phantasmatic, since they are never the things but only their impressions, which were depositing themselves upon the *tabula rasa* while we were indicating.

Therefore indication in the present is at the same time a retention. It is the case of the *Philebus* (34a–b): retention is the safeguarding of sensation, and in a complex way – that of a teleology which is transformed into archaeology – its possibility and resource. Retention offers, in fact, the possibility of that 'differing in the same' which Hegel presents in his *Aesthetics* when, in the discussion of Egyptian art, he says that death happens twice, the first time as death of the natural, the second as birth of the spirit (*Werke*, ed. Michel

---

[3] *'Immantinente'*: 'immediately', 'at once', from the Latin *in manu tenente*, holding in the hand; cf. *maintenant* in French. *'Seduta stante'*: 'immediately', 'then and there'; literally, 'during the session itself' [Eds].

and Moldenhauer, XIII, p. 451). What Hegel means is that a selfsame event is saved as sensible and passes into the intelligible through a retention that produces sensibilization on the one hand – the embalmed pharaoh – and idealization on the other – the first announcement of the immortality of the spirit, i.e. of spirit *tout court*. But this differing in the same is also the history of sensation and, in the mode of a transcendental aesthetic, history as sensation: one perceives as sensible, one retains as intelligible. The same movement characterizes the Hegelian doctrine of subjective spirit (and thus the tradition, of Wolff and of Aristotle, to which this doctrine is heir): *aisthēsis* is saved in retention and, in this way, is also the wholly other, idealization.

3.   'This'

What has been silently introduced (or rather had been tacitly presupposed) in the analysis of indication we sketched in the first section, and then by the examination of ontology traced out in the second, was a certain power of retention, and thus of temporalization, which was posited as the condition of indication of the properly present. But it now appears that this 'time' is sublated [*aufgehoben*] precisely because it succeeds in its intent: 'present' is that which I point out as simply present, without even posing the problem of what may be the *time* in which I indicate it (a problem that may arise in the case of accumulations of perceptions, as in the phenomenon of *déjà vu*). It is obvious that it is the present, given the fact that I am indicating it: just consider, for example, Ryle's great determination, in *The Concept of Mind*, to hold fast to the distinction – which is empirical, though he takes it as transcendental – between seeing and remembering; the fact that the same assumption is at work in Austin's doctrine of linguistic acts is the result of a common ancestry, going back to the Aristotelian critique of anamnesis, for which knowing – as present – and regaining knowledge of something known previously, are not the same thing.

But this very critique is rife with problems. Aristotle writes (*De Memoria*, 449b 10ff) that there is sensation of the present but not memory, therefore one has no memory when one looks at an object that is present, nor when one contemplates it with the spirit; likewise, Aristotle continues, there is expectation of the future, and there is no memory except of the past. From this it follows that only beings endowed with memory have memories, and that they remember with the same faculty with which they have awareness of time. It is not difficult to see the tangle in which these assertions are caught up. The faculty with which we have awareness of time is *koinē aisthēsis*, the synthetic nexus that is at work in every single sensation (if I did not retain something, I would have no sensation of it either); time, in fact, is the number of movement in respect of before and after, and is thus an aesthetic formation in the eminent sense. Now, it would be very difficult to say that the animals that have no memory have sensation, if indeed we have made sensation into something present, as opposed to something past or future. In what sense would theirs be a *present* sensation, and thus a sensation *tout court*, if they cannot distinguish it from the past and from the future? The *nyn* as presence of the present finds its resource and definition precisely on the basis of that which it is not – the past and the future – and which makes it possible. This is even clearer on the objective plane: in what sense could I say that an event is such, and is present, if I do not compare it with a previous state in which it was not? The definition of 'event' analytically implies the intervention of memory. Through the hyperbole/hyperbola of presence, Aristotle not only renders problematic the presence of sensation (the very animals that, devoid of memory, would live only in the present, would never be in the present), but he gets himself entangled in an aporia of memory: do we remember a thing, or the affection it produces? In both cases, if we hold fast to the determination of sensation as that which happens in the present, both the remembrance of the thing and that of the affection turn out to be indiscernible with respect to *aisthēsis* in the proper sense. Quite rightly, Kant (*Critique of Pure Reason*, A 99) affirms that a representation, if it were contained in an instant – if, that is, it were hypothetically placed outside time – would be nothing but absolute unity. Devoid of the *temnein* of time that by positing the discontinuous in the continuous broaches retention, it would not even be sensation; it would not permit us to distinguish the sensing from the sensed (if, as Aristotle does, we assume that in *aisthēsis* the animal and the sensation become one and the same thing); it would not qualify as an event in time (from a before to an after), nor even as something determinate in space – presenting itself, perhaps, as a boundless flash.

It is as if Aristotle assumed, at one and the same time, that the ontological quality of a thing (presence/absence) depended upon the time in which it is apprehended, and that time adhered to things. The aporia of memory, which proves to be indistinguishable, *de jure*, from sensation, is an eloquent sign of this situation. Now, to make clear what is at stake in the 'this-present', let us go back to the mental self-observation suggested by Locke in his *Essay concerning Human Understanding* (IV, 2): there is a difference between *this* sun that I see with my eyes at noon, and the sun I remember with my mind at midnight, and which can be no other than *that* sun. That which renders that sun such, that which makes it *this* or *that* sun, is its presence or absence to perception – not a faculty of the soul but rather a property of being, and specifically of *sensible being*. The reason why this recourse to sensible being is necessary is stated by Kant in his transcendental topic against Leibniz (A 268/B 324ff): we have to distinguish the source from which something we know has come to us, whether from the intellect or the senses; in default of such a topic, Kant continues, Leibniz and his followers have homologized all knowledge, turning sensation into a sort of confused intuition, and have postulated a continuity between sensation and intellect. The result is that for Leibniz 100 ideal thalers are equal to 100 real ones, precisely because they are equal in concept. (But could it also be said that they are equal in intuition? The *form* of the 100 thalers is equal.) The distinction between the true and the false coin is not self-evident, however, because it is made in the world and not in the soul, and has therefore not yet got round the hypothesis of the evil demon. For this very reason, in his commentary on the above-mentioned passage in the *Nouveaux Essais* Leibniz's position with respect to Locke is very realistic. As we have seen, if one remains on the plane of an analysis of the faculties (as Locke does), there is no way of distinguishing intuition from sensation, since their difference lies in things (presence/absence) and not in the soul. One can, at most, observe that in perception and in the other operations of the soul there are necessary connections; in other words, one could say that a grammar regulates inscription on the *tabula*, independently of the existence of objects.

It is typical that, in his reply to Locke, Leibniz has recourse to a scriptural image. Metaphysically speaking, it is not unlikely that there should be a dream lasting a lifetime (i.e. that a mental state should proceed coherently independently of constant references to an external world). Perhaps it is less likely that letters thrown together at random should give rise to a coherent text; the probability is very low, because one begins with a purely stochastic aggregation. Thus in the first case the *tabula* can proceed to the aggregation of a text that makes sense, in a hallucinatory schematism. Small wonder if, within the framework of 'empiricism' (where recourse to the evidence of consciousness is given priority), Berkeley's *Treatise concerning the Principles of Human Knowledge* reached conclusions not unlike those of Leibniz, likewise on the basis of an examination of internal difficulties in Locke, in the same way as his *Essay towards a New Theory of Vision* had contested the positions of Malebranche and Descartes. In the first case, particular events act as simple references for a system of general ideas that is structured in the same way as the Platonic system; in the second, the properties of space are not objectively intrinsic to the external world, but only act as signs and reminders. *Esse est percipi* is the form of all immaterialisms, by no means conflicting with the idea that all sensations are true. On the contrary, it is the correct resolution of that idea, but only when one assumes that some form of writing is already ensconced in perception – an assumption that, in a milieu dominated by the *tabula rasa*, is not surprising.

The use we have made here of a Kantian vocabulary will not appear inappropriate if one considers that Leibniz is enunciating a principle that Kant will not contest, but indeed will wield with still greater prowess: syntactical consistency comes not from things but from traces, which can also proceed phantasmatically, extending the faculty of the imagination to retain the trace without the object of perception. Now, on the level of traces, the difference between full presence and its mnestic or imaginative modifications is wholly ungroundable. If Kant underlines the need to have recourse to a transcendental topic, it is precisely because, at the level of traces, there is no way of deciding – no way, that is, of maintaining that the principle of reason determines things (ontology). The schemata do not produce reality; simply, they make experience possible; small wonder then that in Kant one has such an acute sense both of the value of final jurisdiction of ontology (its irreplaceability and non-constructibility) and of the role of retention as constitutive of experience.

So, when I say 'this', as immediate as my impression may appear to me, I am following a script, which is still at work when, twelve hours later, I say 'that'. Isn't this exactly what is at work when Hegel examines and contests sense-certainty in the *Phenomenology*? If the Hegelian analysis is of such vital importance, this is expressly due to the fact that, in it, philosophical reflection on the *this* is explicitly welded to the theme of writing. The norm of sensation is retention, which is then the way in which Hegel affirms and denies the validity of sense-certainty, through a scriptural example repeated three times, in which the truth of sense-certainty is refuted and confirmed precisely by the inscription of the perceptive given. It is the experiment suggested by Hegel: propose to a prephilosophical man – who swears up and down by the value of sense-certainty – to write his certainty down. If it is night, he will write, 'Now it is night'. Twelve hours later it is day. The *this* of sense-certainty, the now, is no longer true, and is saved only as syntactical consistency, to become true once again twelve hours later, like a stopped clock, which nonetheless has the right time twice a day. But the writing upon which Hegel bases his contesting of sense-certainty is also the rule of truth: not of the truth of what is referred to by the *this* (which is emphatically invalidated), but rather, as we have seen, of retention. This is so in two senses. On the one hand, retention appears as a term super-ordinate to the truth or falsehood of sensible perception: the *this* of sensibility has vanished as present perception, but remains as inscription. On the other hand, the new *this* (now it is day/now it is night) ranks as temporality on the basis of a sum of retentions. Indeed, the twelve hours that separate day from night extend as temporality by virtue of a retention, and the this of day or night ranks as present in reference to a past that takes the form of an internal script, simply extended or illustrated experimentally by writing on paper.

This is why Augustine's argument in the *Confessions* contesting the spatialized time of the stars does not appear to be as cogent as Heidegger, in particular, believes. It is true that a man was able to ask God to stop the course of the sun, and time passed even if the sun stood still. But time passed precisely because a *continuum* of events was in course, and thus the Aristotelian value of temporality as the number of movement in respect of before and after was in no way altered by the stopping of the sun. The measure of tem-porality results from the coincidence of a dual simultaneity: that of outer movement, on the plane of what Peirce called world-sheet, and that of inner movement, on the plane of the soul conceived as a place of forms and *tabula rasa*. This means that time originates precisely in the inscription of the trace; i.e. at the moment in which the two movements come to coincide, in a single and simultaneous instant, in a *hama*, in an 'atom' of space and time together like the adverbiality that designates it, in which the outer sheet is impressed on the inner. As we have seen, in fact, not only the *this* (presence) but also the *now* (present) results from inscription, that is, it offers itself as a performance of the trace. And, as we saw, this bi-univocal correspondence comes

from Kant: on the one hand, for experience to be possible
(i.e., for it to present itself as *continuum* and temporality,
giving the *this* and the *now*) it is necessary that the soul
should retain; on the other, the soul retains, and conceives
itself as flux and time, precisely through the postulation of
a fixed and external world with respect to which time can
be conceived as time. It is the argument produced in the
confutation of Descartes (B 274ff), which seems to assume
a superiority of spatiality over temporality, contrary to Kant's
customary position, but which in fact shows a co-generation
of space and time. In Kant's case too, as in Aristotle's before
him, it is not a question of wondering whether there is a
movement in the soul, but rather of asking oneself whether
the origin of temporality and movement (thus, also of
presence beyond the fleetingness of sense-certainty) may be
offered by the general retainability of the trace – by the
meeting of the two sheets.

4.   Writing

A corollary. In *Consequences of Pragmatism* (1982) Rorty,
for his division between 'Kantians' (scientific philosophers)
and 'Hegelians' (hermeneuticians and deconstructionists),
puts forth a notion of writing that is not analysed any more
deeply than his philosophical emblems are: the Hegelians
write, while the Kantians assume that philosophy, in principle,
does not have to be written, insofar as the ideal is ostension.
But – keeping in mind what we said about indication – this
is just the point. If by 'writing' one does not mean the
empirical act of writing – say, alphabetically (and thus
transcribing speech) – but rather the system of retentions
already at work in sense-certainty, and the present indicative at work in ostension, then Kantians or Aristotelians are
no less 'writers' than Hegelians are. Even if we discount the
fact – empirically anything but adiaphorous, even if referred
precisely to what is generally taken to be writing – that,
of the 'Kantians', Quine has published more than twenty
books and Husserl wrote 40,000 pages in shorthand, while

Hegel – in his lifetime – published very little (less than Kant, for example), the burning issue is that, whether 'Kantian' or 'Hegelian', whether philosopher or not, even whether human being or not, every being endowed with retention writes incessantly, since thinking and perceiving are like drawing a figure – like tracing a line while retaining the points. The additional circumstance of taking writing in an extremely strict sense, and of taking up a fundamental scepticism about the possibilities of a philosophy as the mirror of nature, means, then – in Rorty's interpretation – that the 'Kantians' have renounced ostension, while the Hegelians, writing, share and ratify Rorty's scepticism, so that theirs is nothing but a literary writing. In other words, Rorty tells us that the 'Kantians' have renounced writing, except for a few short articles, which moreover are useless (either because they are superfluous with respect to ostension, or else are absolutely worthless, ostension having shown itself to be a fleeting dream), while the 'Hegelians' dedicate themselves to writing long unhinged novels, wasting their time devastating the few things written by the 'Kantians', who in turn have absolutely no desire to write. But neither an artist nor a philosopher (nor, for that matter, any man at all, who in everyday life is in fact extremely demanding) would be satisfied with a limitation of this sort, which deprives them in principle of the possibility of saying something true – although it does console them, assuming that not one of their propositions can ever be falsified either, because the game that has been opened is one in which everybody wins.

Nevertheless, we think we understand how Rorty came up with the idea that the 'Hegelians' were unrealistic: it is no doubt true that these 'Hegelians' insist upon the 'constituted' character of presence – a fact that, indeed, appears to be a harbinger of immaterialism. The fact is, however, that the role of 'constitution' is part and parcel of the phenomenologies of perception, which soon enough conclude that the way in which the truth of sense-certainty is affirmed refers to the indubitable forms of an impression, rather than to the presumption of existence of what exercises that impression. According to the formulation of the

Theaetetus (191ff), taken up by Aristotle (*De Anima*, 424a 17–20, *De Memoria*, 450a 31–2), and later by traditional rhetorical psychology (see, for example, Quintilianus, XI, 2, 4) – and which underlies the gnoseological value of the *tabula rasa* – that which is impressed in the mind understood as *tabula* or block of wax is not the iron or bronze of the ring, but rather its imprint. This consideration blurs, in particular, the differentiation between *aisthēma* and *phantasma*, because, on the basis of this reasoning, *aisthēmata* themselves are in no way more material than *phantasmata*.

II

1. Form

As a student of philosophy at the lycée Louis-le-Grand, Derrida 'wrote essays described as "Plotinian"' (Bennington, p. 328). Now, a cardinal statement of the *Enneads* (VI, 7, 33) runs: *to gar ichnos tou amorphou morphē*. Although Derrida explicitly quoted the passage only twice (*Margins of Philosophy*, pp. 66, 157), in a number of ways the principle regulates all his reflections: form is that to which the index refers and it constitutes itself as presence, as *this* sensible or intelligible, but, in its presenting itself, it is from the 'beginning' the *ichnos* of a non-presence that heralds and recalls its other. *Forma* is the Latin for a complex of Greek values running the gamut from pure *eidos*, to *morphē* as involved with and opposed to matter, to *schēma*, which holds for both the visible and invisible, according to the alternative, still in force in Bacon, between *schematismus patens* and *latens*. In Cuvier, Geoffroy Saint-Hilaire, Thompson d'Arcy, *schēma* is form as principle of the intelligibility of an object, but already in Plato it is connected with both *eidos* and *rythmos*, which explains in what sense there can be a form of time. Form is seen, but also heard (the refrain, the sonata form), intuited and thought, presenting itself as a covert and invariant structure, which is thus irreducible to the pure dimension of the image; Mach is perfectly right when, in *Contributions to the Analysis of Sensations*, he holds fast to the distinction between *Gebild* (image) and *Gestalt* (form).

As we see – and note how naturally we pronounce this 'we see', transposing it from the sensible to the intelligible – the quarrel between the presence and absence of images in thought is nothing but a misunderstanding of the notion of *eidos, morphē, schēma*. As if it were a question of opting, say, for metaphors alone against concepts alone, and above all as if it were possible to isolate a definite notion of metaphor or concept, according to the ingenuous perspective stigmatized by Derrida (*Margins of Philosophy*, pp. 207ff): *eidos* and *idea* have the same root, *vid-*, and the distinction between the eyes of the body and those of the spirit seems to come *after* this primary identity. Thus it is not a question of unveiling the metaphorical origin of the concept, or vice versa, but rather of illustrating how metaphor and concept stem from an originary retention, in which there is no distinction between metaphor and concept, but none between nature and culture either, if 'metaphorical' tropism may be considered the same as in the sunflower [*girasole*, turning towards the sun], the heliotrope, according to the motion of the sun from Orient to Occident.

The force of written metaphor (supposing one can speak of metaphor at all, since it would be necessary to indicate a proper name; let us say, rather, the force of written catachresis) is due to the fact that it gathers in itself all the values we have recapitulated. Writing is the trace of speech, but is also what preserves the essence of speech beyond temporal discontinuity; it is what vanishes in the comprehending it has made possible (according to an image that runs from Plotinus to Dilthey: the letters vanish when the spirit has been understood). Inventing writing, then, does not mean making a radical breach in the history of culture, but rather reflectively formalizing a schematism and a transcendental aesthetic that have been at work ever since the most defenceless of impressions. Writing means making a note in an agreed-upon manner of what otherwise has to be remembered (*nota*); transcribing something said in words (alphabet); learning one or more characteristics of a thing represented (ideogram); producing a mediation between concept and percept (example, schema, symbol); retaining in general (where explicit writing would be nothing but a reflective formation, like number, of the transcendental ichnology at work in the act of perception whose first manifestation we saw in the 'this'). Writing proper, in the terms we have recapitulated, carries out a function that is not primarily literary, but is related to the possibility of stopping time making it possible, so as to ensure a correlation and a transition between the sensible and the intelligible.

In our examination of writing, however, it may be useful to begin with the example of mnemotechnics (i.e. internal writing), rather than with the pages of the *Phaedrus* that tell of Theuth's invention, external writing. What Simonides, the inventor of mnemotechnics, discovered was that whoever wishes to retain her memories has to *transform them* into images and arrange them in mnemonic places; the places stand for the order, and the images (*notae*) for the things to be remembered. The process is double: objects are transformed into psychic *notae*, with a passage from sensation to intuition, from *aisthēma* to *phantasma*; the *notae*, however, are rationalized and operate diagrammatically, without the icon's having to maintain a figural likeness to what, instead of being represented, is now retained (with a passage from intuition to reasoning). The analogy between material writing and mental writing is confirmed by the fact that, in telling of the invention, Cicero specifies that the places rank as the wax of the writing tablet and the notes or simulacra as letters (*De Oratore*, II, 86, 354). What we have, in short, is another version of the *tabula rasa*, and at this point we have to wonder – in line with the impossibility of considering writing as a metaphor with a sense of its own – whether perception, of which the writing tablet is normally taken to be a metaphor, is simply illustrated by the example of writing, or whether writing, in some deeper sense, describes the characteristics of perception.

What would appear to be the shortest bridge between the experience of internal writing, as a reduced illustration of perception, and external writing, is traditionally ensured by the polarity – and, more deeply, by the complementarity – of hieroglyphics and the alphabet. Phenomenological evidence tells us that hieroglyphics are not purely sensible – not any more so than the alphabet is purely intelligible; they are both phenomena of inscription of the sensible which, in a primary and in fact already reconstructive phenomenology, is transposed into the intelligible. This circumstance on its own justifies the continuity between hieroglyph and alphabet. Many of the alphabetical signs come from hieroglyphs (indeed, according to Warburton's hypothesis in *The Divine Legation of Moses Demonstrated*, Moses defaced the Egyptian hieroglyphs out of obedience to the commandment, 'Thou shalt not make unto thee any graven image'); which is a mirror image of the case where, in a language, letters are used in a merely iconic way (T-shirt, T-bone steak, U-turn, V-neck, Y as a figure of doubt), or where one uses acrostics or painted words, or spells words by saying A for Albany or Andy, or aberrantly re-phoneticizes abbreviations (okay, deejay, jeep, veep, teevee). And then there are the cases in which the alphabet becomes a codebook where the letter acts as a symbol, which goes to show that the alphabet not only derives from the hieroglyphic but can also return to it. Now, however – and this is the third term that regulates reversibility – we have to note a crucial circumstance: this 'return' is not a going back to the origin, to the pictogram, from which the ideogram and, finally, the phonogram derive. If that were so, we would have to assume that the earliest rock-painting was perfectly realistic, when vice versa the first manifestation of drawing is constituted by the inscription of points and lines (with which Euclid's *Elements* begins: which, moreover, in beginning with a negative definition, that of the point as what has *no* part, partially cuts down to size the widespread conviction that the ancients, unlike the moderns, privileged the positivity of an order given in nature). In other words, that at the origin there is a realistic image that is progressively weakened on its way towards the alphabet is a myth that is fundamentally empiricist (from image to *logos*, originary version of the consolidated schema and yet marked by the fragility of a 'natural' passage from *mythos* to *logos*), and that not only cannot account for what ensures this transition, but does not even pose the question.

The situation is further muddled by the fact that the progressiveness of the alphabet with respect to the hieroglyph may be accounted for if both are taken to be nothing but a secondary expedient of a primary orality – as if peoples without (empirical) writing also had no transcendental writing (i.e., no aesthetic and no logic), its place being entirely taken by language. In an adventurous return to the origins, one thus ends up supposing an initial state in which something perfectly aniconic (speech) is opposed to something absolutely iconic (image), without considering that, as we have seen, the finger that gives a sign towards the thing, linking it to sound, already acts as a form of writing. This is particularly clear in Gelb's *Foundations of Grammatology*, where the primacy of orality is simultaneously a supremacy of the pictographic, almost as if the history of writing described the tortuous route by which image and speech, initially separate, are ultimately united in the alphabet, in the same way that Babylonian arithmetic and Greek geometry are ultimately conjoined in algebra (when the conjunction has been made possible by a common ichnological origin, already at work on the plane of a transcendental aesthetic). Thus, according to Gelb, all writings – which regularly succeed a state of primary orality – have a single origin, the proto-Sumerian pictographic, which gave rise to Sumerian cuneiform (and thence the Akkadian and the Elamitic), the Egyptian pictographic (at the origin also of the Semitic syllabaries, thence, by evolution, of the alphabets), and the proto-Elamitic pictographic (at the origin of the Chinese pictographic and the Japanese syllabic, with the mediation of the proto-Indian pictographic – a conjecture eruditely derided by Voltaire, since it would have made Chinese and Mexican into the same language). In sum, at the origin, but *already* after speech, is the image and the rebus, i.e., the imperfect way of making an alphabet phonetic. After all we said at the beginning about the 'this', the problem here appears to be different: it now consists in describing the process by which an act of archē-writing, i.e. indication, gives rise to the two parallel series of language and writing.

Gelb supposes, then, that language comes long before writing, developing into pictures (which are not writing) before taking on the more clearly defined forms of semasiography (first descriptive and then identificative, which is where mnemonics comes in) and, finally, phonography (as full writing, according to the further internal stages of word, syllable, alphabet). But if systems of signs have their *telos* and their final consistency in the word, it is because Gelb assumes that language is the real thing, while writing is its picture, according to a thesis that, in Gelb's opinion, would not be invalidated even by those cases – which are recalled in the *Foundations* – of non-phonetic elements in alphabetic writings ('Mr. Theodore Foxe, age 70, died to-day at the Grand Xing Station'), which are not probatory (in the same way as algebraic signs) because always virtually reversible in a language. What we see here, in short, is glaring confusion of language and code; Gelb is so well disposed to the alphabet – no less than Theuth was to the hieroglyph – that he neglects some elementary circumstances. Try, for example, to solve *linguistically*, through *logos*-language, such a simple operation as 3 × 3. Observing that it can be phoneticized into 'three times three' certainly does not demonstrate that phoneticization is of much help in getting to 9 (or 'nine'); rather, it is a help in showing that, precisely because the access to number is not linguistic, what is needed is mnemonic learning of the multiplication tables. This does not hold only for mathematics, or for other forms of specific notations such as music, but is at work at the very heart of so-called alphabetic writing. Look at the keyboard of a computer, where, besides letters and mathematical numbers and symbols, there is a series of values (punctuation marks and other signs that *are not* rephoneticizable: /:/ signifies 'colon' in a completely different way from how 'A' signifies 'A') that are really and truly ideograms in the alphabet: \, !, £, $, %, &, /, (,), =, ?, [,], *, +, @, #, §, ,, ;, :, ., -, _, <, >. Thus the functioning of an alphabetic writing not only does not explain the totality of the ichnological operations at work in writing, but – what is even more decisive – an alphabetical writing cannot be explained by a recourse to *logos* (understood as language) alone.

But looking at it the other way around, not even a purely ideographic system is truly self-consistent. If the key to the deciphering of the Egyptian *grammata* came from the full recognition that they could also have an alphabetic value (and thus required the postulation of an underlying language, Coptic), contrary to the old beliefs that considered them purely ideographical symbols of an extremely ancient wisdom (Kircher), or – based on the same principle, but with a negative slant – as the deformed wreckage of a boundless antiquity (Vico), this does not mean hieroglyphics were only alphabetical, but rather that they were superordinate to the distinction between phonogram and ideogram. It is the doctrine Champollion expounds in the *Grammaire Egyptienne*: hieroglyphs do not only have mimetic or figurative values, but can also act as tropes or symbols (and so a 'theorem' can also count as a 'mnemoneum' [aid to memory]). And in virtue of their value as tropes, where, for example, the part counts for the whole, it is not surprising that hieroglyphs can also count as 'signes de sons'; that is, can be used as an alphabetic value that designates the sound of the initial of the thing depicted. Precisely because there are never images as such, there are never letters as such, nor is there – as we have just shown with the example of the computer keyboard – a purely alphabetic writing.

This thesis calls for a supplementary observation regarding the inconsistency of a pure iconicity, which is no less improbable than a primary orality. In fact, already on the level of mime, a hieroglyph is not the detailed representation of a single object (a photograph is not one either, if only because it is the two-dimensional presentation of a body that is often three-dimensional); furthermore, pragmatically speaking, the *sign* (because, on the basis of what we have said, the hieroglyph is already a sign – a value of 'mnemoneum' that ensconces itself at the heart of a theorem) is utilized with a diagrammatical function; that is, it serves to indicate, say, *all* vultures, and not only *this* vulture. In other words, the process that leads from mimesis to the metaphor of the alphabet has been programmed ever since the mimetic (aesthetic or theoretic) level. The upshot here is that, if on the one hand we cannot posit an absolute division between hieroglyphic and alphabetical, on the other (coming to questions of aesthetic and logic) the process that leads from mimesis to the trope and thence to the alphabet (or, following the Kantian distinction between different types of hypotyposis, from example to symbol to schema) is not represented, for example, by the Humean process perception/imagination/idea (meant to express the passage from full presence to enfeebled image, to still further abstraction), precisely because at the level of full presence a prescription of signs was already at work. Here, what poses a problem, or at least directs our attention, is the value of primary representation as *re*-presentation. But if this is true – if every form is *ichnos* – then what institutes the *referential* nature of the trace?

2. *Name*

When Hegel, in the doctrine of subjective spirit in the *Encyclopaedia*, places intelligence immediately after mechanical memory, he is clearly not formulating an empiricist thesis; he is, in fact, insisting on the marvel innate in the doubling by which, from the iterability made possible by retention (which, as such, has nothing of the empirical or the transcendental), the freedom of the intelligence can emerge. This circumstance was even more manifest in Warburton (taken as a model by Condillac, who in his turn, as we shall see, is often the palimpsest of Hegelian semiology), who, in agreement with Bacon, notes how writing originates with neither the ear nor the eye, but with the gesture; which is to say that speech and writing are not mother and daughter but – in a way that is difficult to conceive – are sisters, outcomes of an aphonic trace that places itself at the origin of two series: on the one hand, time, speech, spirit as the logical presence of consciousness present to itself; on the other, space, writing, *aisthēsis* as aesthetic presence that speaks to the eyes and ought to find its truth in the spirit. The same situation is already to be found in the *De Interpretatione*, one of the most ancient grammatologies we possess: the afflictions of the soul, which express themselves in speech and letter, find their resource (their institutive middle term) in *symbola*; that is, in the *notae* and traces that transform intention into expression.

These circumstances afford further proof of the isomorphism between writing and the transcendental aesthetic. Where iteration is concerned, the so-called 'rationalist' tradition is mirrored in that of 'empiricism'. In Wolff's *Empirical Psychology* the passage from the lower cognitive faculties, of sensible nature (sense, imagination, *facultas fingendi*), to the higher (attention, reflection, intellect), takes place in memory as the faculty of retention, and the two parts, the inferior and the superior, are as many specifications of a single cognitive faculty. On the other hand, Hume treats the expectation of similar cases as a possibility of prevision, *and therefore of science* (which, to be sure, is not a merely psychological or regional ambit). In discussing this doubling it is difficult not to think of the *Aufhebung*, and to wonder whether its initial form is not, precisely, the imagination as that which retains sensible provenance in idealization. The big problem – and great resource – concealed in this doubling all come down to the question of retention: as reception of form without matter, retention is the possibility of sense; but, to the very same extent, it is the origin of idealization – and thus the possibility of the intellect. It is not fortuitous that the question of memory has traditionally represented a major challenge for philosophical reflection. Memory, like retention, is the sensible and its possibility; but it is also the intelligible, and is part of intelligence. Above all, however, if we work backwards, we observe how memory cuts across the distinction between sensible and intelligible, precisely because it is what makes both of them possible.

Explaining intelligence with memory, and memory with the hypothesis of permeable or impermeable neuronal traces, will therefore not be so coarsely positivistic, unless positivism is backdated to the point where it becomes contemporary with ancient metaphysics. In the *Posterior Analytics*, Aristotle observes that the beginning of animal intelligence resides in the trace of sensation: the origin of *logos* – soon cancelled, since sensation will turn to the particular object, and *logos* to the universal (87b 37–8) – is the persistence of an inscription (*monē tou aisthēmatos*, 99b 36–7) that, vanishing as sensation, is saved as intuition, positing itself at the origin of *technē* and *epistēmē* (and of *logos* itself, if indeed the possibility of a code – i.e. of a language – is iterability, and thus, preliminarily, retention). This means that, in an animal that is mute but not devoid of memory, at the first level of sensation we already find writing. As we know, to ground the implication of intellect in the sensible – and, reciprocally, the doubling of the sensible in the intelligible – Aristotle has recourse to the hypothesis of *two* intellects and two memories: passive memory, and reminiscence that functions as a syllogism, actively seeking traces of what has been remembered. They are substantially the same as Hegel's two memories, the lower (*Erinnerung*) and the higher (*Gedächtnis*). Between the two stands representation (*Encyclopaedia*, §451) as remembered intuition, the middle point between freedom and an intelligence still chained to the here and now. *Remembered* intuition is thus placed in the transition between the intuition chained to the sensible and the emancipation *implied by memory*, through which representation fluctuates freely, and this fluctuating, the outcome of passivity, *is freedom*, which, as release from the sensible, is nothing but the repetition of the trace. Between the first and the second memory there is nothing but a doubling; that is, the transition could not have taken place without retention. This is to say that the surpassing of an *aisthēma* in the *phantasma* that preserves it is intramnestic, and, reciprocally, that freedom is nothing but doubling; from representation Hegel in fact goes on to thought, which is placed under the sign of repetition. Thus §465 of the *Encyclopaedia*, after the treatment of iterative forms, such as memory in its two specifications (the sensible and the spiritual, the one coming from the senses and the other related to thought to the point of self-identification) and representation, begins the section on thought in the same way as in Wolff and Condillac, reunited at least by the hypothesis that the sign functions according to a process of N + 1 (it is not a sign the first time but is one the second, which means that the first time of a sign is, simultaneously, a second time). Hegel writes, 'Intelligence is twice' (*ist wieder*, i.e. *iter*, is iteration), in the same way that Condillac observes that a man, if he were not capable of signs, would be an imbecile, without considering the fact that what is essentially proper to man is at work in the animal that follows a trace or trail. The position of the intellect is therefore problematic – because, on the one hand, it is a question of showing the intellect as the repetition of the sensible, but, on the other, this repetition also presents itself as a complete alteration. Thought, even in its most hyperbolically speculative form, originates from memory, reflects something, iterates it, and preserves it. Parallelism and doubling, as a technical function that ensures the transition from lower to higher, is in fact a duplication and an iteration that is inferior twice over: once because it takes place in the empirical (the empirical that is extinguished), and once because it operates empirically (the trace that is iterated).

So in the beginning, and ever since sensation, there is not *logos* or image but trace. This is the basis of the Platonic doctrine of the soul as a book – at first alphabetic, and then, if necessary, ideographic, or even realistic, as in a film; but it is above all the basis of what, paradoxically, induces Hegel, in the *Encyclopaedia* – which is to say, in a grammatology that is also a psychology and a transcendental aesthetic – to formulate the most powerful commendation of alphabetic writing. The point is of the utmost importance – because if one were to demonstrate that there is a reversibility of hieroglyph into alphabet *and* of alphabet into hieroglyph, then it would be clear that these two performances are not posited as nature and culture, hologram and image enfeebled to the point of abstraction, but rather as the two perform-ances (one more sensible, the other more intelligible) of a selfsame trace that has made both of them possible from the very beginning.

Let us sum up Hegel's arguments with extreme concision. It must be said that, at first blush, they do not seem the least bit logocentric: space is superseded and preserved in time (which indicates a primacy of consciousness and speech), just as the sign is cancelled in comprehension; hence we have the primacy of intention, also as intonation (the tone of voice – as in Condillac – manifests the intention of consciousness); the excellence of a language resides in its lexical and morphological universality and simplicity (modern languages are simpler than ancient ones); the sign is always secondary and derived – it is a minimal and accidental part of a language while phonic language is originary, and strengthens its archaeological priority with a teleological superiority that renders alphabetic writing, the shadow of speech, in and for itself the most intelligent, just as Greek art is more open and eloquent than the unconscious symbolism of Egyptian art, which represents a spirit that has not yet attained the reflective clarity of consciousness.

But it is precisely at this level that the apparent inversion takes place, leading to the hypothesis that – true to our description in the previous section – a function that is alphabetic without being logocentric (let's say mnemoneutic or ichnographic) is what, from the beginning, has made the hieroglyphic hypothesis possible. At the end of §459 of the *Encyclopaedia*, in the passage that most radically affirms the inferiority (and heterogeneity) of the hieroglyph with respect to the alphabet, Hegel observes that, among the limits of hieroglyphics and ideograms in general, is the fact that they do not proceed through an analysis of sensible signs, as alphabetic writing does, but rather through an analysis of representations (i.e., they refer to the ambit of *notae* and not to language). With regard to the progression described above, it is specified that the superiority of the alphabet is of an instrumental character. In sum, following the Cartesian argument, just as the hand (symbol of reason) surpasses the limbs of the animals (emblems of habit and instinct), because it is prehensile and at one's disposal, and thus able to perform diverse functions while organs and habit are capable of only one, so the alphabet is more prehensile than the hieroglyph. The latter, which represents a single thing (but we have seen the intrinsic limit of this analysis), cannot bend to the needs of an evolved society, and so is fit for a stationary and scantly innovative civilization such as the Egyptian, and later the Chinese. Now – Hegel continues – in modern times, even in the region of sense such things as muriatic acids have undergone several changes of name. Accordingly, there is always need of a language capable of adapting itself to the manifold necessities of a spiritual evolution that cannot be expressed by a single characteristic. The alphabet, being progressive, avoids the faults of the hieroglyph while retaining its merits, since the habit acquired in reading means that we do not read alphabetic writing as representing speech but, instead, look directly at what is written; which 'makes it a hieroglyphic writing for us'.

The richness of this passage makes it a true sketch of transcendental logic and aesthetic. *On the one hand*, Hegel has passed – without accounting for it and, apparently, without even realizing it – from hieroglyphic to ideogram, from the Egyptian to the Chinese; that is, from the presumed sensuality of the Egyptian (which he condemns in his *Aesthetics* as not fully capable of recognizing the spirit as different from the flesh) to the intellectuality of the ideogram. One may object that, in the Hegelian hieroglyph, the Celestial Empire is even more backward, Asiatic and sensual than the Egyptian Kingdom; but at this point one would have to explain why the Chinese, closer to the rising of the sun, wrote in *ideograms* – in, that is, the very form of sophisticated character that was capable of seducing the *intellectualism* of Leibniz, to whom Hegel explicitly refers in this context. In this 'anachrony', and in the unrecorded shift from percept to concept, from representation of the thing to representation of the idea, Hegel has demonstrated *in re*, and apparently against his own intention, that the alphabetic *is already* in the hieroglyphic, in concept if not in fact – the lack being due to an empirical or instrumental failing, not one of principle. *On the other hand*, as Hegel observes, the multifunctional prerogative of the alphabet would be curtailed if (as with the ancients and the barely literate) reading meant syllabifying, i.e., laboriously going back from letters to sounds, hence from sounds to mental images. Nonetheless the same flexibility that imposed the invention of new things, and so of new words, also facilitates a silent reading, where what is

written is no longer understood as a succession of letters,
but is assumed within an overall reading that isolates names
– which, then, are thought *as names*, and not as mental
images. In other words, on the one hand, *habit* leads us to
use the alphabet as a hieroglyph, according to a clear process in our everyday experience. Errors in the reading of new
or foreign words are due to the assimilating force of habit,
which is instead the rule and positive possibility of a fluent
reading; analogously, in the case of writing, handwriting,
becoming progressively idiomatic as one grows older, often
turns into a kind of shorthand. On the other hand, that
which an ideographized alphabet refers to – not unlike the
hieroglyph – is not an individual *eidos*, nor a representation
either, but rather something that is highly abstract and deeply
asemantic: the *name*.

'We *think* in names' (§462). This means that alphabetic
writing is ultimately understood as a hieroglyphic writing
that constitutes, together, the truth of hieroglyphics and the
truth of the alphabet. A cultured person no longer reads
alphabetical writing as a transcription of speech, nor as a
way of regularly re-creating a mental image, precisely because
she thinks in names and not in images; this, in the next
paragraph of §462, leads directly to Hegel's critique of
mnemonics, which – in his highly reductive interpretation
– traces aniconic memory back to the iconism of a theatre
of memory. A literate person makes use of writing as of a
perfect automatism – which is what led Wittgenstein to
observe that only in the schoolchild learning to write do we
see the work of the spirit. The reading of a cultured person
is thus closer to nature (closer, say, to the myth of the
hunter following traces) than is the *Buchstabieren* of the
beginner. In fact, saying that we think in names, not in
figures, nor even in words as a continuous flow of speech,
means, for Hegel, signalling the extent to which (as we
mentioned) Condillac's *Essay on the Origin of Human Knowledge* constitutes the palimpsest of these passages of the
Encyclopaedia: everything begins with an iteration; what at
first was nature receives, from its first repetition, the value

of culture. The name, as union of visible and invisible, would thus be the end of a process that is already ichnological at the beginning: there is not – as Rousseau, distorting Condillac, will claim – an originary cry that is expression as such, prior to any scriptural interval; if the cry expresses, it is because it repeats. (By the same token, Heidegger's hypothesis – a hyperbole of Rousseau's – of an 'originary word' is absolutely untenable; this word is originary only because it fits into a discontinuum already begun, within which it inserts a caesura; therefore it is writing, and eminently so.) Alphabet and hieroglyph find their truth in a third, which is the schema or the name – that is, a new metamorphosis of the finger and the hand – and so not only does the alphabet come from hieroglyphics but, also, hieroglyphics come from the alphabet. Hegel claims, as Condillac did before him, that we think in names, which are the abstract trace that can then be specified in alphabet and in hieroglyph, just as we perceive through the schemata. In the two cases, we have to do with an exemplarity in which the individual, as *casus datae legis*, goes towards the universal. This, paradoxically, is the reflection the configuration leads us to. Because, faced with the alphabet, we have two possibilities. We can put it forward as a patent schematism, and so trace sound back to the alphabet, and the alphabet to the image. But we can also keep to a level of trace that is prior to the distinction between speech and image – in the trace of a name that becomes thought, and that 'means' nothing (i.e., cannot be traced back to the phonetic dimension of the alphabet).

Here we have the convergence of the eidocentrism that induces Leibniz to praise hieroglyphics and the logocentrism – far more temperate than in Rousseau and Heidegger – that induces Hegel to praise the alphabet. But if this final convergence is possible, it depends on the fact that has been incubated it from the beginning. This is, precisely, the case of the treatment of hieroglyph and alphabet in the *Nouveaux Essais*. On the one hand, Leibniz writes that the hieroglyph seems to be the invention of a deaf person (Gerhardt, V, p. 108); on the other, he recommends its use because it

suggests thoughts that are 'less deaf and more verbal' (ibid.
p. 379). How is this possible? The fact is that on the first
occasion, i.e. in the relative proscription of hieroglyphics,
with 'hieroglyphic' Leibniz was referring to the writing of
the *Chinese*, saying furthermore that it 'fait l'effet de nostre
alphabet'. This is to say that the supposed pictogram and
the supposed ideogram, the presumed *aisthēma* and *noēma*,
are in fact performances of a transcendental finger and hand
that come before the distinction between image and speech,
and that for this very reason can – as is effectively the case
– perform the pragmatic duty of the alphabet, which in its
turn is nothing but a transcription of speech, which is itself
no less subordinate to indication and grasping than the pictogram and ideogram are. The case is no different in Hegel,
who takes up the most negative of Leibniz's determinations
– namely, that the hieroglyph ensures what, to put it
baroquely, *is a deaf reading and a dumb writing*. But isn't
that exactly what happens in the silent reading and writing
of the alphabet for all literate people? And, beyond culture
and unculture, from the beginning and for everyone, isn't
that what happens *in thought*? It is quite true that, thinking
in names, for the name 'lion', according to the example in
the *Encyclopaedia*, we need an intuition neither of the animal
nor of its image. But when, in the *Aesthetics* (*Werke*, ed.
Michel and Moldenhauer, XIII, pp. 394ff), Hegel speaks of
the duplicity, and indeed of the multiplicity immanent in
every image insofar as it can be a symbol (detaching itself
from immediate intuition, of course it still ranks as an image,
but not as the representation of an individual or a class),
the example he chooses is none other than the lion, which
ranks not only as the image of an animal, but also as a symbol
of strength and regality. Whoever takes a lion to portray a
sovereign is already thinking in names, and would do so even
more if, as in the mnemotechnical devices (which are never
purely pictographical, as Hegel assumes), she made use of a
lion [*leone*] to remember not just any sovereign, but Leone
Isaurico or Leone XIII [Leo the Isaurian or Leo XIII].

3. *Logos*

A second corollary. It is symptomatic that, historiographically speaking, in *Of Grammatology* (1967) we find a statement by Madeleine V. David affirming that the nineteenth century, the century of the great decipherings, made a clean slate – *tabula rasa*, the term couldn't be more fitting – of all past reflections on writing, the written character, the hieroglyph, that had come down through Western thought, culminating in the seventeenth and eighteenth centuries. Even more symptomatic is that David recalls how this concealment was not accidental, but rather was eminently favoured by our being alphabetical writers, tendentially inclined to assimilate writing to speech, making the first a mere prop or transcription of the second. This explains in what sense a phenomenon that became explicit in modern times was already prepared for by the Platonic condemnation of writing and why the frequent references to grammatology (Gelb's *Foundations*, as we have seen, is paradigmatic) are steered by the idea of the alphabet as the perfection of writing. The ingenuousness of these thematizations is further evidenced by the fact that the assertion of the perfection of alphabetic writing (its spirituality) is regularly accompanied by an opposition – altogether secondary and derived – between hieroglyph and alphabet, seen as phenomena opposed and historically distinct within an evolutionary course, when in fact they are dependent variables (together with mathematics and the phenomenology of perception, for example) of a general ichnology.

After Rousseau, the world of signs vanishes in the face of a generalized linguistic holism. We can understand why it is of fundamental importance for Derrida's philosophy to recognize the fallacies and contradictions of a thought that dreams presence and the present while turning its back on the conditions of their arising. The general form of this repression, where the Freudian term ranks as *terminus technicus*, is the circumstance where, in the *Essay on the Origin of Languages*, Rousseau recognizes, in Baconian fashion, the natural priority of gesture as the first form of communication – only to subordinate it in short order to the axiological (which

becomes chronological) primacy of speech as the vehicle of
feelings. The myth of the originary, which Rousseau embodies
better than anyone else, in its simultaneous constitution of a
nature and a culture that conceal their scriptural origins, is
the dream – improbable from the perceptological level on
up – of a presence that is full, forgetful, unbroken and uncut.
It is not really so strange that Nietzsche, who (it's true, in
the last years of his life) will make Rousseau and George
Sand the paradigm of all modern evil, in his philological and
Wagnerian beginnings had completely embraced (through the
dream of an indistinct Dionysian upon which the Apollinian
arises) the very thing that, in his maturity, he will shower
with abuse. And if Derrida, in his youth, is tormented by the
divergence between his two heroes, Rousseau and Nietzsche,
it's true that the settling of the quarrel consists in saying
that Apollinian and Dionysian, form and the formless, are
locked in combat even *before* history (*Writing and Difference*,
1967, pp. 28ff); but that, as long as there has been history,
there has been nothing – and by analytic definition – but
form, i.e. discontinuity and caesura.

This said (indeed, for this very reason), we can well understand the reason for linguistic inflation. Language is not
linked instrumentally to the human sciences but is in fact
their condition of possibility, especially once it has been
assumed that language is what is proper to man, that an
animal could never speak, that every trace is oriented towards
the *logos* – in its secondary and derivative sense as language
– as towards its proper *telos*. Despite its reference to the
sign, the pansemiotic moment, in its twentieth-century
resurrection, is a panlinguistic moment. This is not only
because one source of its revival is the linguistic matrix of
Saussure, but also because its overt reference to Peirce has
left in shadow the non-linguistic eventualities of the sign.
This repression is glaringly symptomatic in psychoanalysis,
where linguistic holism is summed up in Lacan's statement
– so widely received and so little reflected on – that the
unconscious is structured as a language. Augustine's *verbum
cordis* is neither Greek nor Latin, nor does it belong to any
other language (*De Trinitate*, XV, 10, 19), and it suspends

all difference between a parodied Cartesian philosophy, based on internal and external evidence, and a hermeneutical philosophy, rooted in the opacity of language: while the limits of language are easily seen (indeed, they are continually thematized), it is more difficult to discern the limits of the trace, and this constitutes a grave objection to the claim to universality of hermeneutics.

III

1. Line

In what sense do the limits of the trace seem impassable? The Hegelian *this* (the first writing, source of all the others, if it is true that the root common to all languages, before the Babelic confusion, is – according to the perpetual attempt to return to the origin of language – 'tik', which indicates both the index and the number one) reveals itself to be a close relative (in fact, the twin) of the Aristotelian *hama* discussed by Derrida (*Margins of Philosophy*, pp. 29ff), and which is met with twice in the passage (*Physics*, 219a 3–6) where Aristotle maintains that we experience movement and time simultaneously [*hama*, together], according to a spatiotemporal simultaneity (*similis/simul*) that is repeated right down to the detail of the adverb of space and time 'together' (*zugleich*) in the first *Critique*, in one of the many passages (A 33/B 49–50) where Kant confirms the correspondence of time and space as forms of sensibility, as attested by the fact that we have to represent time, which as such is invisible, by a line traced in space. Now, if the outer and figurative form of time is represented by a line, this line does not supervene after consciousness but rather constitutes it, being the unity of consciousness in the concept of the line; the schemata, as forms of time, result from this fundamental configuration of the line. Kant, in fact, does not limit himself to saying that we represent time through space (B 154), and that this representability demonstrates that time

is not an ideality but rather a form of intuition; he also says
that to know a line in space I have to trace it (on paper or in
thought, on the outer or the inner tablet) and, *above all* (B
137–8), that *this* line is the unity of consciousness in the
concept of the line (the instituting of the two tablets, inner
and outer, at the first tracing). Here is what is proposed
through this scriptural catachresis: on the one hand (against
Husserl), the trace is more originary than phenomenological
originarity; on the other, the trace is not produced by a
cogito, but produces it. This is Kant's position, emphasizing
(and after having spoken of the tracing of the transcendental
imagination, in a passage, §24 of the deduction in B, that
includes two references to the line of time) that we know
ourselves only as phenomena.

The union of space and time is, apparently, in space and
in *aisthēsis*, but according to a synthesis that is no more
spatial than temporal, no more aesthetic than logical. Kant
writes that the *ich denke*, before the phenomenon (i.e., the
way in which, already in *aisthēsis*, the *ich denke* represents
itself), is a thinking, not an intuiting (B 157). We may ascribe
to this same logic Kant's objection to the fact that Aristotle
includes in the *Categories* modès of sensibility such as *simul*
(i.e. *hama*), or – and each of them would merit detailed analysis, since they are all implicated in the aesthetico-logical
act of the *this* – *quando, ubi, situs, prius,* and even an empirical
mode such as *motus* (B 107, A 81–2). It will be recalled,
however, how Kant, who maintains that such modes have
no place in the family tree of the intellect, remarked that
the tracing of the line is the genesis of consciousness, which,
phenomenologically, is always consciousness of something.
Now, for example, can the trace, which both comes from
the *this* and makes it possible, be considered in the same
way as a pure mode of sensibility – assuming that such a
thing has ever existed? Aristotle gives us an analysis of *hama*
in chapter 13 of the *Categories*, where we read that objects
are called simultaneous that are generated at the same time
(14b 24–5; definition repeated in 15a 11–12). In a certain
sense, then, the *gleich* in question is less the contemporaneity
of points in space, different from the successiveness of points

in time, than it is the simultaneity of space and time, their common genesis, which at the same time (*hama*) is at the origin of consciousness. It seems that Kant has turned the *tabula rasa* upside down, or turned it inside out like a glove. The *tabula* is now not the mind but the world, on which the mind, unifying, traces cognitions in the manner of a geometrical projection. As in Copernicus the apparently objective motions of the fixed stars and the sun are mere appearances due to the projection of our motion in the heavens. The schematism would be an act of inscription that institutes the *tabula* and its content at the same time – the mind and the world, the synthetic unity of apperception and the cosmological totality of the perceived. Tracing the phantasm one institutes presence.

2. Tabula

The *tabula* is often understood as a metaphor of perception: atoms detach themselves from objects, passing through the eyes or, if finer, through the pores. It seems a rudimentary explanation; as a matter of fact, it is unacceptable. It fails to explain how the atoms are detached (Lucretius suggests it is due to the heat of animals, but in that case we should not be able to see inanimate beings), nor does it make clear what guides their trajectories (for example, in the street I ought to see the simulacra in transit at the crossroads, and instead I only see the ones in front of me). And even supposing that all this can be accounted for, there is still the problem of where the synthesis and depositing of the image takes place. Theophrastus, criticizing the atomistic doctrine, points out, among other things, that it is unclear how it happens that I can perceive several things, or remember them, without creating a heap of images outside or inside me. If the *tabula* wants to be a good candidate for explaining perception (which indeed it is, if even today we speak of cerebral engrams), preliminarily it has to explain retention and cancellation. It has to tell us how it happens that a sensation is impressed while the wax remains virgin (avoiding accumulations of perceptions).

In 1895 Freud and Breuer reformulated the demand, saying that the mind has to function like a photographic plate and, at the same time, like the mirror of a telescope. First resolved by Freud in physiological terms, in *A Project for a Scientific Psychology* [*Entwurf einer Psychologie*, 1895] (there are two types of neurons, one impermeable, the other permeable), the question will find its definitive formulation thirty years later, in his *Note on the Mystic Writing Pad* [*Notiz über den 'Wunderblock'*], which explains cognition by analogy with a slab or block where one writes with a point that presses together a transparent sheet and the wax surface beneath it, and where the writing can be cancelled by simply raising the covering-sheet. 'Freud's' model, which Derrida concentrates on in *Writing and Difference* (pp. 196ff), is superior to that of Democritus. First of all, it rules out the possibility of heaps of icons, since Freud, like Plato, does not speak (any more) of images, but of writing. A picture gallery fills up too quickly, perceptions (not only visual ones) have to be deposited in a compressed form – that is, as writing. For this retention to accomplish its purpose, two types of cancellation are necessary. The first is the presence together of mirror and photographic plate, i.e., of reflection that keeps the tablet virgin and retention that makes experience possible, of which Freud speaks and which is resolved, exactly as in Plato, through recourse to the scriptural valorization of the *tabula*. For Plato (*Philebus*, 38e–39b) our soul resembles a book, upon which, first, a writer records *logoi*; only later, in going from the trace back to a mnestic image, does a painter transform the inscription into figure. It is no different in Freud: the soul is not a picture gallery but rather a scriptural support, a book, in which the icons are deposited in a compressed form. But behind this cancellation there is another, more decisive one, by which the acts of constitution withdraw in the face of the presence to which they gave rise, exactly as in the transcendence of the image towards reality, discussed by Sartre (following Husserl), and the transcendence of the present in the face of the presence to which it gave rise.

Now, it is well known that Aristotle, as we saw, not only thematizes the role of the *monē tou aisthēmatos* in the constitution of experience, but writes in the *De Anima* (429b 30–430a 3) that the intellect is in potency all intelligible things, but in act none; just like a tablet on which nothing is written, exactly as would be the case in a *topos eidōn* – in that *chōra* we shall come to in a moment. Put in these terms, however, Aristotle's formulation is not entirely clear, because it draws all the attention to the moment that follows, in which the white page is filled. And this, in fact, made it possible for Thomasius, on the basis of that vision, to justify on Aristotle's authority an empiricism that, at bottom, re-stored the *tabula* to its original (and insufficient) percepto-logical version. Apart from this hardly reliable hypothesis, ancient and modern interpreters (with few exceptions) go back to the interpretation proposed by Alexander of Aphrodisias. Trendelenburg insists on the fact that receiving is a capacity, and that the *tabula* is therefore not to be understood as mere passivity, which in his opinion is how Leibniz interpreted it. The assertion is questionable, because retention is prior to activity and passivity (and thus there is no reason to deny that *Theaetetus* 191 and 195 is the pre-cursor of the *tabula* of Aristotle: Plato's block of wax is indeed passive, but it also performs the most powerful ab-straction, obtaining form without matter). In sum, it is not a question of thinking about the *tabula* – that was Leibniz's objection to Locke in the *Nouveaux Essais*: no tablets have ever been found in the soul (Gerhardt, V, pp. 99–101) – but about the retention it represents; this is the argument with which Hicks and Rodier approve Alexander's reading.

For the Aristotelian Exegete *par excellence*, the material intellect (*nous hylikos*, Aristotle's *nous pathetikos*) resembles the 'tablet's not being written', where the soul acts as a material support, and the 'not being writen' is in the intel-lect (ed. Bruns, 84, 20–5). The intellect is pure potency of inscription, and therefore is not affected; it is form in the sense of formatation, a retainability prior to the distinction between active and passive (85, 1–10) that takes the form of a 'middle voice' (the term Derrida applies to the 'action' of *différance*; see *Margins of Philosophy*, p. 9); it is passive insofar as it receives, but active insofar as a retention is preliminary to perception, is its condition of possibility. In short, unwritability is a capacity of [retaining] only insofar as it is in the first place a capacity for [retaining]. Just as the abstraction performed by sensibility is the greatest abstraction possible, since it ensures the radical judgement that separates form from matter, so the 'passivity' of retention is also the greatest possible activity, since it originates all the operations of both intellect and sensibility: perception in the present and of the present, the synthesis of complex forms, memory, reasoning, etc.

Differences aside, in Alexander we are very close to Leibniz, who grants Locke that nothing is in the intellect that is not in the senses, provided one admits the clause: except the intellect itself. The best of the examples Leibniz uses to illustrate his thesis (Gerhardt, V, p. 132) is this: one may certainly assume, with Locke, that our mind is like a camera obscura, as long as it is granted that the back surface has creases, which produce modifications (which explains why the selfsame impression can please or displease). If – against Leibniz's intention – one hypothesizes that the folds are only aggregations of memory, then, strictly speaking, there is nothing innate except for the disposition to receive impressions. This version is nothing but the other side of the principle that – as Kant writes (A 102n.), presuming originality – the imagination already comes into play in perception, with the possible outcome (which Kant does not dwell upon) that seeing and pretending are the same. Now, what is of interest here is that the *tabula* explains not only perception but also (as in our earlier discussion regarding the line) the arising of consciousness itself. At the origin of both *aisthēsis* and *noēsis* there is a retaining that comes before perceiving and thinking. At this point, it can also be assumed (in agreement with Leibniz, who in §§26 and 27 of the *Discours de Métaphysique* affirms a congruence between the *tabula* and anamnesis) that the superimposing of impressions is more cancellation than inscription, since it scratches and cleans off a palimpsest (or, if you prefer, a 'scratch card') from which will emerge the full face of truth; or else, as Hegel hypothesizes (*Encyclopaedia*, §464), that the tangle of inscriptions facilitated by the youthful quickness of the memory ends up by saturating the *tabula*, leaving it, in later life, a naked and absolute recipient of pure being and pure space in which true objectivity can emerge.

What all these avenues cannot exclude is the absolute reign of retention; as Bergson put it, no habit is inevitable, except for the habit of getting into habits, the first of which, if we think about it, is temporality as constitutive of experience. After all, of the three types of a priori/a posteriori enumerated by Aristotle – according to nature, according to the order of knowledge, according to time – the decisive characterization, the ultimate matrix, is indeed the temporal, because the difference between *ta saphēstera tē physei* and *ta saphēstera tē hēmin* is already given in time – a time that, like the movements of the soul, is no more empirical than transcendental, since it is a pure 'potency' of retention, which is in turn undecided between active and passive. As Spinoza said, if a stone that is falling could think, it might think it was doing so freely. Of greater interest, however, is the question put the other way around: how far is passivity passive? And when does activity begin? How far is a wax tablet inert if, without it, there would be no retention?

3. *Chōra*

Let's take the next step. The soul receives form without matter – but what becomes of the matter? And – this is even more complicated – in what sense would this forming be *producing* (or – not the same thing – *constructing*) matter? *Constructio* is Latin for *syntaxis*, according to a grammatical and grammatological value, similar to Leibniz's example, of written characters as the measure of reality; the concept of archives is also a percept of archives, in the sense that the archivability precedes the concept, but also the percept, making them possible. Vico, in the first discourse of the *De Antiquissima*, dedicated to Paolo Mattia Doria, theorist of synthetic geometry, advances a thesis we find later in Kant, and that opposes those who wanted to demonstrate existence mathematically (specifically, the existence of God, but that was not the principal concern): while the demiurge moulds in three dimensions, the true human is in only two dimensions, like a *monogram*. This is how the difference between production and imitation is already determined in the *Republic*: the divine bed, recaptured by the craftsman, is one we can walk around; the painter's mimetic bed only gives us an image, which is always the same. It is exactly how Plato describes writing in the *Phaedrus*, where moreover, as in the *Timaeus* and the *Republic*, writing is compared to painting, which would seem to speak but in fact does not, just as the sophist can neither answer nor ask, but 'booms out like a gong when it is struck' (*Protagoras*, 329a). Here 'speaking' is to be understood not as an opposition between *logos* and writing, but as an alternative between the living and the dead; writing is the evil, but, at the same time, the good that opposes it is the living *logos* – that is, according to a metaphor that was already commonly used by the tragedians, the *logos* written in the soul that apprehends (*Phaedrus*, 275c–276b). It may well be, then, that the idea is like a writing, only it has to become *living* writing, just as the categories have to be realized in phenomena through the schemata. To understand this, it will be useful to follow the different meanings of a term Plato used quite often, especially in the *Theaetetus* and, above all, in the *Timaeus*: *ekmageion* (tool, implement, apparatus).

In the *Theaetetus*, the *ekmageion* is precisely the *tabula rasa* (191c 9: *kerinon ekmageion*), the wax support in the soul understood as a book, on which impressions are deposited. This retentive function is met with on one of the occasions in which *ekmageion* appears in the *Timaeus* (75c 2), where the word refers to the spleen, which keeps the mirror of the liver always bright. Thus in the first case it is the photographic film, in the second the mirror of the telescope. However, with a movement analogous not only to the schematism but also to the process that will lead Kant, in the *Opus Postumum*, towards the search for an ether, that hypothetical and problematic substance which permits the articulation of the schema as far as the individual, *ekmageion*

is not only the *tabula* but also the impression deposited on
it. In the first case, then, the *ekmageion* indicates a certain
retainability (or cancellability); in the second, the trace of
an existence. This is how it appears in the *Theaeteus* (194d
6, e 6), related to *sēmeion* and in a context where Plato
systematically uses the word *ichnos*. Given these assumptions,
it should not surprise us that *ekmageion* will come to express
not only the receptivity of the *tabula* and the impression
deposited on it, but also the third that makes the application possible, according to the use of the word in the *Laws*,
where it designates the schema (*ekmageion te tritou*, 801d
6–7) that figures as the character (*typos*) necessary for the
practical application of the *nomos*.

The *tabula* as *ekmageion* thus plays all the roles: it is
retention, impression, constitution. Now, in the *Timaeus* –
arguably the most immediate precursor of the *Schematismu-
skapitel* – formless *ekmageion* (48e 2, 50c 2, 51d 1) is defined
as *chōra* (58a 8 and 58d 2), which presents itself as a *third*
type, different from the intelligible, eternal and immutable,
which acts as a model (*paradeigma*), and from the sensible,
ever changing, which is its imitation (*mimēma*). Already at
this level we should take careful note of the point that it is
difficult to think this 'third' precisely because it precedes
aisthēsis, which has a late genesis (43c 6), and so what
phenomenologically is first comes last in the creation of the
world, and comes from the 'third' – from the synthesis made
possible by the *chōra* (31b 8). Sketching a familiar schema:
if the model is the father and the imitation is the son, the
chōra is the mother, 'invisible and formless species' (*anoraton
eidos te kai amorphon*, 51a 7). Now, when Plato speaks of
the *ekmageion* he is describing something that is both inside
and outside the soul – a wax that is superordinate to both
the soul and the world. It is thus perfectly natural that
Alexander should have recourse to the *ekmageion* to charac-
terize the material intellect, as a substrate that does not
identify itself with any of the things it can think (*De Anima*,
84, 15–20); likewise, it is predictable that (Taylor *ad
Timaeum* 50e 1–4) there be a clear echo of the *ekmageion* in
the *De Anima* of Aristotle, both in the assumption that the

intellect is potentially all the beings that it knows (429a 10ff), and in the affirmation that sense is potentially all the percepts (418a 3). Invisible and insensible, polymorphous and obscure – and therefore, as Derrida observes (in *Khōra*), exorbitant with respect to the very determination of mother or matrix – the *chōra* is thus the pure potency of retention that is at the origin of all construction. Indeed, with a line of reasoning that stays close to the *Timaeus* and the *De Anima* simultaneously, Plotinus explicitly grounds the parallelism between soul and *chōra* in the fact that both are potentially all things (*Enneads*, II, 5, 5). The soul and the world arise together, on the basis of an act of retention that creates time, i.e., the number and size that gives form to things (III, 6, 18; this will be the *nous morphotikos* in Proclus' scholia to the *Cratylus*). Thus the universal matrix is also Cronus who devours his children, because everything is born and perishes in time, which, as such, is the insensible sensible. The obscure and imperfect existence of time – of becoming, and of *aisthēsis* that is never given as such – finds its Archimedean point in the soul, which does not limit itself to apprehending, but constructs in the strong sense – not in the sense of producing matter, but in the sense of *syntaxis*. Constructing time, the soul traces the line, which in turn posits the sensible and the intelligible, the schemata and the forms – and, by a strange temporality, posits the soul itself, which begins to exist in the first act of retention.

Keeping in mind what we said earlier about the 'not being written' of the *tabula*, writing is a metaphor that is not alexandrine [refined, decadent] but Alexandrian [after Alexander of Aphrodisias]. It is clear that Socrates does not condemn writing in the name of the *logos* but is calling for another writing, that fully meets the needs of Platonic mathematicism. This can be verified from several points of view. In the first place, *logos* does not mean dialogue, as has generally been assumed since Schleiermacher, but rather, in mathematizing form, relation or proportion. (It is by far the most prevalent value of the Greek *logos*, as opposed to the Christian *verbum*.) The interlocutors in the Platonic dialogues are as many mathematical relations, one larger, one smaller,

etc., and, exactly, as *logoi*, they *measure themselves* against
one another. (Thus, in the *Republic*, Plato proposes an algo-
rithm to demonstrate by how many times a tyrant is unhap-
pier than a king; by the same token, at the beginning of the
Parmenides he seems to establish a precise relation between
Parmenides, who is 65 years old, Zeno who is 40, and Socrates who 'is still very young' – in a certain sense, Socrates is
the *logos* that makes it possible to measure Parmenides and
Zeno.) Then again, writing is presented as a systematics of
relations at the moment when Theuth presents his inventions
to the Pharaoh, as is shown by the fact that the discoveries
in question are all mathematical or, more precisely, make
the continuous discrete: music, trictrac and mathematics
(in Egyptian mythology Theuth in fact was considered the
inventor not only of writing but also of mathematics). In
sum (no doubt paradoxically), Plato is not a theorist of the
sciences of the spirit (and typically the praise of dialogue
cannot be taken, as regularly occurs in those sciences, for an
apology of literature – which, indeed, Plato condemns), but
was able to pass for a mathematizing *Schwärmer*. Now, like
mathematics and like perfect memory, internal writing reaches
its perfection only at the moment of *application* (which is
why a writing that remains only external, or inert, is con-
demned as asthenic: but it is also the asthenia of the *logos* of
an inept man who wishes to be an adviser to the king; or,
again, the asthenia for which physicists traditionally reproach
mathematicians).

With this in mind, it is interesting to note the inflation
of writing, along with its valorization, which – against other
and more widespread perspectives in Plato – characterizes
the *Timaeus*, i.e., the discourse on genesis *par excellence*. (1)
At the beginning of the dialogue (17a 1–3) allusion is made
to a fourth [guest]. In this 'fourth', whose identity is not
known, there is the exorbitant character of the *chōra*: the
absent fourth, whose part will have to be played by Timaeus,
has been affected by *astheneia* (17a 4), which is the pre-
dominant character of writing in the *Phaedrus*. (2) A little
further on (19b), the contribution to the theme of the *Republic* offered by the *Timaeus* is asserted on the basis of the

argument (which in the *Phaedrus* and the *Republic* refers to writing) that the description of the ideal state seems like a painted animal, to which one would like to give existence and life (just as writing seems to be alive but is not, so it is with pictures of the mimetic). (3) Then (22b ff) comes the story of ancient Egypt and of the dialogue between Solon and the priests of Saïs that Critias claims to have heard as a child from his grandfather. The gist of the myth is that what seems to be immediate evidence is nothing but a mediation that has been forgotten, just as the floods devastated the archives of the Greeks. Thus the critique of writing in the second scene is transformed into praise, as is also demonstrated by a linguistic detail: Critias says he remembers the story well because he learned it in his childhood as a game (*paidia*, 26c 1). Now, in Plato *paidia* normally indicates writing, which – paradoxically – is regularly connected with old age; in short, *paidia* is the game of the elderly. Thus in Hippias's derision of mnemotechnics (of writings that are internal but inert), which produces genealogies that delight old ladies (*Hippias Minor*, 268d–e, *Hippias Major*, 285e), so in the *Phaedrus* (276b ff) and in the *Laws* (685a) mnemotechnics is a game that is suitable for a forgetful old man, *tombé en enfance*. Now, in the *Timaeus* – where the Greeks appear to the Egyptians to be perennial children on account of the floods – Critias turns the paradigm upside down (or confirms it): he remembers that story from his childhood very well, as if it had been branded on his memory with fire (26c 3), which is a clear reference to the *logos* written in the soul. (4) The fourth scene of writing is that of Timaeus himself, who tells of the construction of the world from the ideas. Socrates emphasizes the importance of the fact that it is a true history and not invented myth (26e 4–5) – as if to say that after so many false stories about writing, there is a true one at last. Still, one may doubt whether this story is superior to the others, because the culmination of the myth (the construction of individual things) is for Timaeus only a 'likely' [*verosimile*] story – in fact, a myth (just as for Kant chemistry is only an empirical science, and therefore not a true science), and the a priori possibility of the construction (i.e. the non-mythical aspect) is a third that is neither sensible nor intelligible, and which is understood as in a dream. (5) The fifth scene of writing – the material genesis of the world – brings the game of deceit and truth to its greatest tension, since here one confesses to constructing something that in its *telos* is only 'likely' [*verosimile*: 'like truth'], and that finds its possibility in a bastard *chōra*.

4. Geometry

A third corollary. In 'The Origin of the Work of Art' Heidegger, with great phenomenological finesse, describes how the self-consistency of the work gives rise to the setting up of the world and setting forth of the earth; that is, to the genesis of the intelligible and the sensible. It would not be difficult to show that we have to do here with a metamorphosis determined by the *tabula rasa* and by the primary role of retention, since the constructing of the world and the earth results from time; i.e., of the primary retention that cuts (*tempus, temno*: the example of examples presented by Heidegger, before Van Gogh's painted shoes, is precisely a *templum*) the continuum giving rise to that discontinuity on the basis of which experience becomes possible, be it history or nature. That we have to do here with a 'third' is, moreover, confirmed by the insistence on the laceration, the *Riis*, the 'originary' conjunction–disjunction on the basis of which the sensible and the intelligible become thinkable. It is, however, easy to see how Heidegger's version is only apparently audacious, because at bottom it assumes that all this description delineates not the normal state of experience, but rather a specific type of knowledge that is given us by art. Accordingly, either one accepts the fact that with this we have illustrated artistic experience alone, i.e. the Sunday of life that leaves the other six days unexplained, or else one is forced to embrace a panaestheticism that – against all evidence of the senses – declares that reality has disappeared to make room for the virtual and the simulacrum.

Against this peculiar backdrop, Derrida takes as his starting-
point the origin of geometry. Geometrical construction
traditionally has been the model of all constructions, as is
attested by Kant's reference to Thales (B XI–XII). Kant
goes on to illustrate the limits of this constructionism in its
application to philosophy, which is thereby allotted to the
given; in this regard Pascal had already passed his famous
judgement, 'ce qui passe la géométrie nous surpasse' – which
marks the exact limits of human power. Now, Derrida places
the emphasis on how construction itself – geometrical construction included – is circumscribed by an objective limit,
namely, the fact that constructing supposes a minimal act
of retaining. Specializing in the forms of mathematics and
geometry, but drawing its resources from its own origin,
writing appears as the highest possibility of all construction
(Introduction to *The Origin of Geometry*, p. 89). At this
level, retention's role in construction manifests itself first of
all in the problem of the construction of ideality and, even
more, in its traditionalization: apparently, and in their ideal
principle, the Pythagorean theorem and the truths discovered by Euclid are such independently of the forms of their
transmission. And nevertheless (with a movement that seems
to intersect anew with the *De Memoria*), the maintenance
and reactivation of ideal presence comes to depend upon
intersubjectivity, hence on the trace in general. Without
writing, Thales, who studied the power of construction on
the sands of Egypt, would have been confined within his
mnestic finitude (this is the basis of the 'anti-Platonic' discourses on writing in Bacon, Descartes and Leibniz, who
commend writing's faculty of externalizing arguments that
otherwise would encumber the memory and the imagination); and, what is more, his discoveries would have been
threatened by the historical finitude of a man or a generation (before writing, 'l'art perissoit avec l'inventeur',
writes Rousseau in the *Discourse on the Arts and Sciences*, a
theme taken up by Kant in his *Muthmaszlicher Anfang der
Menschengeschichte*).

Apart from the fact, which we still do not find adiaphorous,
that for Derrida the question is not of the origin of art as in

Heidegger, but rather of geometry, i.e. of the *form* of truth
in general, what we have here cannot simply be taken as a
possibility of transcendental historicity. Without retention
we would not only be without science, we would be without the world. The 'act' of retaining is a cutting, it broaches
a discontinuity in a continuous flow that is not yet experience:
the image is that of the routed troops Aristotle presents in
the *Posterior Analytics* (100a 10–15), arguing that the incep-
tion of experience is analogous to the moment when one of
the fleeing soldiers takes a stand and the army comes back
together. Now, in this perspective, the hypostatization of an
originary temporality becomes implausible, because time is
always already second. The selfsame hypostatizing tendency
is to be found in Heidegger – *et pour cause* – in the determination of the transcendental imagination: just as Hegel was
not able to attain an originary temporality but repeated the
spatialized time of the tradition from Aristotle onward, so
Kant – Heidegger insists, in *Kant and the Problem of Metaphysics* – drew back from the abyss of the transcendental
imagination, as the common ancestor of sensibility and intellect. He sees proof of this in the fact that in the second
edition of the Kantian *Hauptwerk* the role of the imagination is prevalently assumed by the intellect. Here Heidegger
fails to consider that the part of the work that remains
unchanged is more decisive, namely the chapter on the
schematism (the pragmatics that is the purview of the imagination); and, above all, that in the deduction presented
in the second edition reference to the imagination as the
faculty that retains perception in the absence of a percept is
a strengthening of the need of retention as the possibility of
constitution. As for the rest, it is nothing but a question of
names: if the imagination as 'third' is, like the *chōra*, a walker-
on that plays all the roles, there is nothing regressive in
assigning it certain functions of the intellect. The fact is that
the third cannot be named – naming it means losing it; which
is why Derrida insists on the fact (*Margins of Philosophy*,
pp. 26–7) that there is no name for *différance*, or that the
pure trace does not exist, *différance* being, from the standpoint of *Of Grammatology*, articulation.

IV

1. Third

In *Faith and Knowledge* Hegel starts off with a critique of Enlightenment finitism (and thus also empiricism), which, however, will lead him to the transcendental determination of everything empirical. Hegel's research, in Kant's wake, is oriented towards the determination of a 'third', which is at the origin of both the empirical and the transcendental. To arrive, truly, at an infinite that is not the shadow of the finite – philosophy's obsession, and not only in empiricism but, typically, in Descartes – what needs to be thought is not the first or the second, but the third that, in its excess, overflows them, according to the definition of the transcendental imagination in Kant, which Derrida takes up in his characterization of the trace. Truth, for Hegel, cannot be deceived by such a 'consecration of finitude' (*Gesammelte Werke*, ed. Buchner and Pöggeler, IV, p. 323). Thinking the third means, then, not returning to the first as presumed ground of the second. The trace, in fact, is not the sensible that is at the origin of the intelligible, but that which is inscribed as sensible and, in the act of inscription, is saved as intelligible (so, as was the case with the tablet and the *chōra*, it would be arduous to define the trace as *eminently* sensible). This, we believe, is what Hegel is referring to when he remarks that in Kant there are two ways of overcoming the finitistic perspective – that of the transcendental imagination (as third, the common source of sensible and intelligible), and that of the deduction of the third category from the first two, in the act of definition of the table of the categories. Behind this praise there is the idea of construction (and the reproach against Kant, which will be repeated in the *Remark* to §262 of the *Encyclopaedia*, for having been too timid in his constructionism); but construction does not come from nothing, it comes from the third, i.e. from retention as its possibility. Judgement, in fact – any judgement – has a subject (which is empirical and particular) and a predicate (which is universal). The synthesis of these two terms is an 'originary' unity.

It is the originarity of this originary that particularly troubles Derrida, who focuses on the problem of how everything can begin with a complication, with a synthesis that blocks the way to a simple origin; this has been Derrida's thesis ever since *Le problème de la genèse dans la philosophie de Husserl* (pp. 12–13), which is in every respect the sinopia of all his subsequent works. The synthesis here is originary retention – the 'not being written' of the *tabula*; i.e. retainability. It is synthesis as synthesizability before being synthesis of *this* or of *that*. As Hegel writes, it is 'absolute synthesis, absolute insofar as it is not an aggregate of random unities', and thus synthetic judgements a priori are possible through the 'absolute originary unity of the heterogeneous' (*Gesammelte Werke*, p. 328). Which is to say, once again, that they are possible by virtue of the retainability guaranteed by a *tabula* that arises in the act of the tracing of a line – a tablet that writes itself writing the world. *But this amounts to saying that judgements are a priori insofar as they are a posteriori*, just as the maximum productivity of the imagination results from its reproductivity that places it at the 'origin' of time. That is why for Hegel the imagination is to be seen not as mediate but as originary – and this is admissible only if, indeed, one assumes the complex character of the originary, which is determined *après coup*. Hegel himself makes this clear when he reproaches Kant for having expressed himself badly, seeing in the a priori a pure unity, 'that is, not originarily synthetic' (*Gesammelte Werke*, p. 330), since the sense of the deduction is to be seen in showing that phenomenon and thing-in-itself exist only in their union – that is, in the convergence, the 'third', of the two sheets of the *Wunderblock*. Kant's merit, then, lies in his having shown how the true form is triplicity, in which the germ of the speculative is deposited, since it is there that one finds both the possibility of duality and 'a posteriority itself', which is no longer 'absolutely opposed to the a priori', which in turn no longer presents itself as empty formal identity (*Gesammelte Werke*, p. 335). This, precisely, is the *tabula* in its Hegelian version: the archē-written tablet, which, by an inflation of traces, returns to virgin wax, just as a coin, by excessive abrasion, regresses to metal.

It is not a question, then, of saying that the intelligible is the shadow of the sensible, but of thinking an exorbitant middle. Every transcendental philosophy is quasi-transcendental, while a philosophy that is 'just' transcendental would not be transcendental at all, since it would not be able to shoulder the burden of its constitution. The question here is of looking time and again at the process, at the *différance* that ensures the transition from finite to infinite, from passive to active, and vice versa. What is interesting, at the end of the line of reasoning we have attempted to follow, is that here, far from attending a consecration of the finite – the only 'consecration' there is – we have to do with a necessary implication of finite and infinite, passive and active, aesthetic and logical, a posteriori and a priori, where neither of the two terms can assume an eminent value: for they are (and the case of the schematism is exemplary) nothing other than two performances of the trace that saves the sensible as it constitutes the intelligible, and from there, once again, through time, ensures the possibility of experience. This explains why Kant can maintain that the imagination already intervenes in perception (and so is a judgement of the senses), *and* that I do not acquire synthesis from experience (because synthesis is itself the possibility *of* experience); that the synthesis of the intellect is only logical (B 152), *and* that synthesis in general is the result of the imagination (A 78, B 103). What we have here is a process analogous to the one that induces Kant, to the astonishment of his interpreters, to say that the reproductive synthesis of the imagination falls within the transcendental faculties of the soul (A 102). But the astonishment recedes if it is assumed that productive and reproductive result from a distinction between a priori and a posteriori that in its foundation is temporal, and that time is a result of the synthesis and the trace. Thus, in the reflective judgement, the object is given first by the law (according to the characteristics of the exemplarity of the example), which in turn broaches a 'singular historicity' (*The Truth in Painting*, p. 51), which broaches, already at the level of perception, that which at the level of consciousness Freud describes as *Nachträglichkeit*.

2. Reason

This 'third' is reason: Hegel, in *Faith and Knowledge*, reproaches Kant for transforming reason too soon into something that is conditioned – that is, once again, into intellect. Now, however, it is a question of seeing to what extent Kant is 'finitist' in this choice. As Derrida observes reading the third *Critique*, intellect and reason are articulated through an intermediate member (*Mittelglied*), judgement (*Urteil*), which, paradoxically, is a part that is both detachable and not-detachable, or, as Hegel would put it, an 'originary part' (*Ur-teil*) (ibid., p. 38). It is evident that what is said of the articulation of reason and intellect also holds for the synthesis of intellect and sensibility through the schematism. This disjunctive synthesis is the work of the sign: a representative, sign or symbol, is detached (beautiful as a symbol of morality, hypotyposis, *Spur*, *Chiffreschrift*, *Wink*), on the basis of which conjunction becomes possible. With good reason Derrida writes, in *Of Grammatology*, that the sense of being is perhaps a determinate signifying trace: a simple present being and, at the same time, the formless it recalls and announces.

Between concept and presentation there is thus established a relation of mutual exchange. It is the case, for example, of the colossal in the *Critique of Judgement*. Here Kant writes that '*Kolossalisch* (. . .) wird die bloße Darstellung eines

Begriffs genannt, die für alle Darstellung beinahe zu groß ist' (§26). The Academy edition, followed by Weischedel, chooses the reading *die* (*Akademie-Ausgabe*, V, 253, 10), while Vorländer accepts *der* (referring, accordingly, to *Begriff* and not to *Darstellung*), because *der* was given in the errata of the first edition, even if the second and third editions retained *die*. Noting this oscillation between concept and presentation, Derrida (*The Truth in Painting*, p. 144) wonders whether they don't come down to the same thing, since the presentation of something that is too large to be presented always produces an inadequation of the presentation to itself. If this passage seems particularly significant – more significant than the beginning of the chapter on the schematism, where Kant writes (B 176, A 137), to the astonishment of some interpreters, such as Vaihinger, who take it for a misprint, that one *intuits* the roundness in a circle and *thinks* it in a plate – it is because here there is no room for any charge of simple empiricism. In other words, saying that roundness is thought in a plate can give rise to a more or less Lockean thematization, for which ideas are nothing but amplified empirical images, which would make thought nothing but the trace of sensation, where, however, attention is focused on sensation, not on the trace. Saying, instead, that in the colossal the representation is inadequate to the concept, or the concept to the representation (as is indeed the case in the relation between aesthetic ideas and ideas of reason), means showing that what presents itself is, precisely, the trace of something formless, which is simultaneously given and concealed in form, according to a process whose functioning is ensured by the trace.

The trace is the *absolute* union (therefore also the absolute disunion, the differential) of sensible and intelligible, and this explains its superordinate value with respect to concept and representation. In Derrida's own words (*Margins of Philosophy*, p. 172n.), 'The trace would not be the mixture, the transition between form and the amorphous, presence and absence, etc., but that which, by eluding this opposition, makes it possible in the irreducibility of its excess.' We said *absolute* union (with all the paradoxes of this bond that unbinds) because *ichnos* comes before *logos*, and also before number, as the nexus of 'everything unlimited that has been bound by limit' discussed in the *Philebus* (27d), and taken up by the young Schelling in his annotations on the *Timaeus*: a third class that, like the *chōra*, 'is not just a mixture of two elements, but is the class of all the *infinite* elements that are bound by the *finite*'. The real and metaphysical opposition between sensibility and intellect, a posteriori and a priori, passivity and activity, and, obviously, finite and infinite, comes from an ichnological absolute, the bondless bond that in *Speech and Phenomena* (pp. 101–2) Derrida sums up in the principle that infinite difference is finite. Absolute finitism, then, which, as absolute, includes its own other. Finitism of a life of pleasure mixed with intelligence in the *Philebus*, as of the identity between bond and bondless in Hegel's absolute, or, in the hyperdialectical language of Derrida's 1954 dissertation, dialectic between the dialectizable and the non-dialectizable.

3. *Absolute*

A last corollary. One may wonder what sense there is in looking for thirds, when all we have to do with are firsts and seconds. In archaic numerations, three designated the unlimited, i.e. all numbers higher than the monad and the dyad (which is why we believe that *tre* [three] has the same root as *trans*). Setting off down the road of the third, don't we make fools of ourselves? According to Diogenes Laertius (*Vita Platonis*, 26), the comedian Theopompus, in the *Autochares*, mocks Plato who spouts 'One is nothing and two is barely one', ridiculing a dissatisfaction with the sensible and the intelligible that was the negative premise of a *Schwärmerei* that was to be unleashed in the *Timaeus*. And then, we may add, ridicule is the least of it; the fact is that the search for the third is dangerous, if one just thinks of the consequences (from the absolutism of consciousness to that of the state) of the Kantian definition of reason as the faculty of the unconditioned. This, too, is why the religion of our times has concentrated on the empirico-finite, the positive, and the given, with some exemption for compulsive supplements of the soul (such as art, regularly taken to be the domain of unreality), and as for the rest has maintained a majestic silence. So, if the invasion of language was the fashion before last, followed by the invasion of ethics, it is because there is a genetic continuity between the two terms. First, with the identification of being and language, any reference to the fundamentally gnoseological value of philosophy is shelved and the foundations laid for the existentialist appeal, in which we inhabit an exclusively human dimension. At this point there is nothing but ethics, politics and history. But in both cases we witness the preliminary putting in parentheses of that which defines the domains of ethics and language as limited. As a result, the unlimited finitism of our epoch preserves an unanalyzed relation with the infinite but refuses to face the problem of the genetic conditions of finite and infinite – except in an appeal to a 'bad infinity' that is in fact a eulogy to the finite. The situation is made worse by the fact that there is not even much cause for rejoicing at the rare attempts to hold fast to the infinite, or to take a look at the third.

'Whereof one cannot speak, thereof one must be silent' – *but*, when this is made into something more than an obvious norm of etiquette, scientific or otherwise, it becomes a saying that is falsely profound, *just because* speaking or being silent changes nothing at all: 'doesn't change a comma', we say in Italian, and the comma is one of the many non-linguistic acts performed by the alphabet. Saying 'whereof one cannot speak, thereof one must write' will change things even less, if by 'writing' one means an empirical performance, which, furthermore, leaves us uncertain as to whether anyone has read it (on the telephone we have no need of confirmation, with a fax it is absolutely necessary). It is not a question of this word or this writing, nor of dallying in occultism, looking into a darkness that, if it is truly and totally so, cannot be mitigated by an adaptation – by the one for which we say, wrongly, that cats see in the dark. Philosophy is thinking what is – or, as we have suggested, what there is –

even if, as is quite probable, in a great many circumstances (and not only in death) knowing it changes nothing; as little as it may be at times, knowing, knowing it, is *something*; this is why philosophy cannot allow itself sham or story-telling. And if Derrida not only coined but also gave the only tenable interpretation of the saying 'whereof one cannot speak, thereof one must write', he certainly did not wish to suggest that this writing is an extreme and rare resource one has recourse to when one is without words, when one is struck dumb before an arcanum; he was suggesting, rather, that we write before and after we speak, in short that we are always writing, even if we don't always know how it happens, just as we continually use our hands, without knowing how they work (and knowing or not knowing it changes nothing). Thinking what is, however, involves – and on this point we are no longer sure we follow Derrida – privileging synthesis with respect to disjunction. After all, we cannot consider a misfortune the fact that dialectic is the absolute master; only for it shall a remnant return. Or, in the Latin of the Vulgate: *Reliquiae convertentur reliquiae inquam Iacob ad Deum fortem* (Isaiah 10: 21).

Bibliography

I. Works by Jacques Derrida referred to in the text (in chronological order)

Le Problème de la genèse dans la philosophie de Husserl (1954, dissertation) (Paris: Flammarion, 1990).
L'Origine de la géométrie, by Edmund Husserl. Translated with an introduction (Paris: Presses Universitaires de France, 1962); trans. John P. Leavy, Jr, E. *Husserl, Origin of Geometry, with an Introduction by J. Derrida* (Lincoln: University of Nebraska Press, 1989).
De la Grammatologie (Paris: Minuit, 1967); trans. Gayatri Spivak, *Of Grammatology* (Baltimore, MD: Johns Hopkins University Press, 1976).
La Voix et le phénomène (Paris: Presses Universitaires de France, 1967); trans. David Allison, *Speech and Phenomena* (Evanston, IL: Northwestern University Press, 1973).
L'Écriture et la différence (Paris: Seuil, 1967); trans. Alan Bass, *Writing and Difference* (Chicago: University of Chicago Press, 1978).
La Dissémination (Paris: Seuil, 1972); trans. Barbara Johnson, *Dissemination* (Chicago: University of Chicago Press, 1982).
Marges de la philosophie (Paris: Minuit, 1972); trans. Alan Bass, *Margins of Philosophy* (Chicago: University of Chicago Press, 1984).
Positions (Paris: Minuit, 1972); trans. Alan Bass, *Positions* (Chicago: University of Chicago Press, 1981).
La Vérité en peinture (Paris: Flammarion, 1978); trans. Geoffrey Bennington and Ian McLeod, *The Truth in Painting* (Chicago: University of Chicago Press, 1987).

La Carte postale de Socrate à Freud et au-delà (Paris: Aubier-Flammarion, 1980); trans. Alan Bass, *The Post Card* (Chicago: University of Chicago Press, 1987).

'Mes chances. Au rendez-vous de quelques stéréophonies épicuriennes', *Tijdschrift voor filosofie*, no. 1, March 1983, Leuven (repr. in *Confrontation* 19, 'Derrida', 1988).

'Bonnes volontés de puissance: Une réponse à Hans-Georg Gadamer', *Revue internationale de philosophie*, no. 151, 1984, fasc. 4, *Herméneutique et Néostructuralisme: Derrida–Gadamer–Searle*, University of Brussels/PUF.

Du Droit à la philosophie (Paris: Galilée, 1990).

Jacques Derrida (in collaboration with Geoffrey Bennington) (Paris: Seuil, 1991); trans. Geoffrey Bennington, *Jacques Derrida* (Chicago: University of Chicago Press, 1992) [cited as Bennington].

Donner le temps: 1. La Fausse Monnaie (Paris: Galilée, 1991); trans. Peggy Kamuf, *Given Time: 1. Counterfeit Money* (Chicago: University of Chicago Press, 1992).

Points de suspension . . . (Paris: Galilée, 1992); trans. Peggy Kamuf and others, *Points . . . (Interviews 1974–1994)* (Stanford, CA: Stanford University Press, 1995).

Passions (Paris: Galilée, 1993); trans. David Wood in *Derrida: A Critical Reader*, ed. David Wood (Oxford: Blackwell, 1992) and in *On the Name*, ed. T. Dutoit (Stanford, CA: Stanford University Press, 1995).

Khôra (Paris: Galilée, 1993); trans. Ian McLeod, in Dutoit (ed.), *On the Name*.

Spectres de Marx. L'état de la dette, le travail du deuil et la nouvelle Internationale (Paris: Galilée, 1993); trans. Peggy Kamuf, *Specters of Marx. The State of the Debt, The Work of Mourning and the New International*, intro. by B. Magnus and S. Cullenberg (New York and London: Routledge, 1994).

Politiques de l'amitié suivi de *L'Oreille de Heidegger* (Paris: Galilée, 1994); trans. George Collins, *Politics of Friendship* (London: Verso, 1997).

II.   Quotations in the text are from the following editions:

Alexander of Aphrodisias. 'Alexandrie Aphrodisiensis Praeter Commentaria Scripta Minora', ed. E. Bruns, in *Supplementum Aristotelicum* (Berlin: 1892).

Augustine. *The Confessions of St Augustine*, trans. John K. Ryan (Garden City, NY: Doubleday Image Book, 1960).

Augustine. *On the Holy Trinity, Doctrinal Treatises, Moral Treatises*, in *Nicene and Post-Nicene Fathers, Vol. 3*, trans. Arthur West Haddan, revised W. G. T. Shedd, ed. Philip Schaff (Massachusetts: Hendrickson Publishers, 1994).

Descartes, René. *Oeuvres de Descartes*, ed. C. Adam and P. Tannery (Paris: Vrin, 1897–1913), 12 vols.

Habermas, Jürgen. *The Philosophical Discourse of Modernity*, trans. Frederick Lawrence (Cambridge: Polity, 1994).

Hegel, G. W. F. *Gesammelte Werke*, ed. Buchner and O. Pöggeler, Academy of Sciences of Rhineland-Westphalia (Hamburg: Felix Meiner, 1968–), 40 vols projected.

Hegel, G. W. F. *Werke in zwanzig Bänden*, ed. K. M. Michel and E. Moldenhauer (Frankfurt am Main: Suhrkamp, 1969–71), 20 vols.

Hegel, G. W. F. *Hegel's Philosophy of Mind, being part three of the Encyclopaedia of the Philosophical Sciences*, trans. William Wallace and A. V. Miller (Oxford: Clarendon Press, 1971).

Kant, Immanuel. *Critique of Pure Reason*, trans. Norman Kemp Smith (London: Macmillan, 1983).

Kant, Immanuel. *The Critique of Judgment*, trans. James C. Meredith (Oxford: Clarendon, 1986).

Leibniz, G. W. *Die Philosophischen Schriften von G. W. Leibniz*, ed. C. J. Gerhardt (Berlin: 1875–90), 7 vols.

Lévinas, Emmanuel. *Proper Names*, trans. Michael B. Smith (Stanford, CA: Stanford University Press, 1996); the chapter 'Wholly Otherwise' is also included in: *Re-Reading Lévinas*, ed. Robert Bernasconi and Simon Critchley, trans. Simon Critchley (Bloomington: Indiana University Press, 1991).

Pascal, Blaise. *Pensées*, trans. Honor Levi (Oxford: Oxford University Press, 1995).

Plotinus. *Enneads*, trans. S. MacKenna, revised B. S. Page (London: Faber and Faber, 1969).

Quine, Willard Van Orman. *From a Logical Point of View* (New York: Harper Torchbooks, 1963).

Wittgenstein, Ludwig. *Philosophical Investigations*, trans. G. E. M. Anscombe (Englewood Cliffs, NJ: Prentice–Hall, 1958).

Wittgenstein, Ludwig. *Tractatus Logico-Philosophicus*, trans. C. K. Ogden (London: Routledge and Kegan Paul, 1983).